A Jewban's Story: the Cuba I Remember

A Jewban's Story: the Cuba I Remember

The Memoirs Of Joseph Shuman

DR. JOSEPH SHUMAN

ISBN-13: 9780692733820
ISBN-10: 0692733825
Library of Congress Control Number: 2016914116
Shuman Publishing House, Baltimore, MD

About the Authors

*J*oseph Shuman, MD, was born in 1939 in Havana, Cuba, and grew up there during the carefree 1940s, 1950s and the turbulent decade that followed. He is an endocrinologist who has practiced medicine for forty-two years and has published numerous peer-reviewed articles in medical journals. Since 1973, he and his wife, Maxine, have resided in the Miami area. They have been married for fifty-one wonderful years and have four children and twenty-one grandchildren. They enjoy traveling and seeing foreign films.

Ian Shuman, DDS, was born in 1966 in Cadiz, Spain. Together with his father, Joseph, he has co-authored this book and authenticated research. He has practiced general, reconstructive and aesthetic dentistry for twenty-five years. Ian has published numerous peer-reviewed articles in dental journals, is the Editorial Director of Continuing Dental Education for PennWell Publishing, and lectures internationally. He and his wife, Stacey, reside in the Baltimore area and together have six children: Daniel, Yoni, Michael, Avi, Zoey, and Shani.

Prologue

When people hear that I am Cuban born and Jewish, they are at first surprised and then curious. "Cuban? You don't look Cuban," they say. "And Jewish. How is that possible? There are Jews in Cuba?" they ask innocently.

Like my parents, many Jews settled in Cuba as a means of escape from the harsh, restrictive, and often-dangerous life found in Eastern Europe during the early twentieth century. For over fifty years, Cuba became a safe haven for those fleeing from pogroms, Bolsheviks, and Nazis. This was due to its quasi US protectorate status after Spain's defeat in the Spanish-American War of 1898.

In his article entitled "Tropical Remnants: The Architectural Legacy of Cuba's Jews," Paul Margolis explains why Europe's Jews fled to Cuba:

> Cuba became a way station into the U.S. in the 1920s, when restrictive laws made immigration into this country more difficult. It was possible to go to Cuba, wait six months to get a Cuban passport, and then go directly to the U.S. Some Jews stayed in Cuba, others were stranded there by even more stringent immigration restrictions.[1]

---

1 Margolis, Paul. "Tropical Remnants: The Architectural Legacy of Cuba's Jews." *Jewish Heritage Report* Vol. I, Nos. 3-4 / Winter 1997-98, accessed June 21, 2016, http://www.jewish-cuba.org/cubarch.html

These are the memoirs of one Cuban Jew and his family's life. The stories told span over a century, cover three continents, six countries, seven languages, and many harrowing tales.

This is my story...

One

1912: Dąbrowa Białostocka, Poland

Nestled in the *shtetl* (village) of Dąbrowa Białostocka was a small two-room home, common for the majority of its poor Jewish inhabitants. It was here that my grandparents, Elizabeth Blancstein-Yaroshevsky and Zev Wolf Yaroshevsky, lived with their three children, Chaim, Friedel, and Leiba. The Yaroshevsky family lived as orthodox Jews, just as their ancestors had done in this tiny border town for over four hundred years. My grandfather was considered a *talmid chacham*—a wise, intelligent, learned man in the Torah.

Due to the deteriorating economic conditions of Poland in the second half of the nineteenth century, many Eastern European Jews were forced into small-scale vegetable farming, my grandfather included. He was a simple farmer by day, and late into the night he stayed up reading the Talmud by the glow of a single candle.

My grandparents' two-room home sat on rich, fertile ground near a small tributary of the Biebrzy River, with a picturesque view of the surrounding green hills and great forests. Being a tiny home, each room was multipurpose. The front of the home served as a shop and dining room by day and my grandparent's bedroom at night, while the second room served as both the children's bedroom and the kitchen.

Even though my grandmother was pregnant with her fourth child, her daily chores continued. Between fetching water from the river's edge, gathering wood for heat, cooking, and caring for her children and their small stock of farm animals, her job as a homemaker was demanding and full time. One evening my grandmother was busy preparing dinner for her family. It was one of my grandfather's favorites, a simple meal of *kasha-varnishkes* (buckwheat and bow-tie noodles) with some salted meat. As she watched over the boiling pot, a severe abdominal pain gripped her. It took her breath away. She knew labor pain; it was all too familiar from her three previous childbirths, and she would soon need help.

In the early turn of the twentieth century, doctors in rural Poland were scarce and medical care was typically "emergency only." Living a near-subsistence lifestyle, the people of these shtetl towns were made tough, and my grandmother was no exception. She knew another contraction would come, and when they became closer, she would call on the town's nearest *akusherkah* (the Yiddish and Russian word for midwife). Until then, she simply continued her cooking chores.

After dinner, she had my grandfather fetch the akusherkah. He hitched a small, weather-beaten wood wagon to his horse and hung two lit lanterns from the top planks, one on each side. He urged the horse on the short trek along the muddy streets that led to stretches of widened game trails through lush, dense forests of oak, maple, and sycamore. After a short while, he returned with the akusherkah. It was Monday, July 8, 1912, and at nine o'clock that evening, Elizabeth delivered an eight-pound baby girl. They named her Sara after a relative who had passed away. It was a way to honor a deceased family member by the same name. However, with Yiddish being the dominant language of European Jewry, she was always known by her nickname, Sortchele or Sorche. To me, she was Mama, and to her grandchildren, Baba Sara.

1912–1925: Growing Up in Dąbrowa Białostocka

As the baby of the family, Sara was pampered but otherwise had a normal childhood. She attended school up to the eighth grade and always excelled in languages and mathematics. In a family of smart people, she was considered a prodigy. Sara mastered several languages, including Polish, Russian, Hebrew, Yiddish, and German, and her skills in

2

mathematics became legendary. She always strived to learn more, but, unfortunately, the gymnasium (high school or school of baccalaureate) was not available in her hometown or any towns within a reasonable distance.

The lack of higher education in these small towns was due to the fact that Poland had been "partitioned," carved up and annexed by its neighboring countries over two centuries. There had been many partitions, but the most significant in this period of time was the partition that challenged the work of the Polish Commission on National Education. Germany, Austria, and Russia sought to destroy Polish national consciousness by germanizing and russifying the education system. During the 123-year partition, pockets of resistance in the Polish Diaspora continued teaching and publishing in Polish, and some innovations such as vocational-training schools appeared.

Between 1918 and 1939, the newly independent Poland faced the task of reconstructing a national education system from the three separate systems imposed during the partition. Although national education was available in the 1920s with the establishment of state universities in Warsaw, Vilna, and Poznan, they were primarily available to the upper classes. To obtain any form of higher education, my mother would have to live in the Polish capital of Warsaw. However, being raised in a poor family, her financial resources were limited, which made this an impossibility. She became frustrated but did not give up on her dream. She knew that someday she would have the opportunity to continue her studies. A mind like hers had to be fed and challenged. Soon it would be.

Two

Wednesday, November 15, 1905: Kovno, Lithuania—"The Pale"

During his childhood, my father, Isaac, had a dark and bleak existence. He offered crumbs of information about his life, but never elaborated. What I can share comes only from my memory, cobbling those bits and pieces together. This is his story...

Isaac Shuman: Growing Up in Kovno

On November 15, 1905, my father, Isaac, was born to Lena Vigoder-Shuman and Yosef Shuman. He was the youngest of five children and lived in a shtetl located within a Lithuanian city. When it was part of the czar's Imperial Russia, the city was called Kovno. The Jewish inhabitants called it Kovne. Kovno was within a region known as the "Pale of Settlement" or, simply, the Pale. The Pale was a border territory that encompassed a large geographic area within Lithuania. It was within this area that Jews were allowed to live, and no further beyond. My father's town of Kovno sat along one of the most northern portions of this boundary, only fifty miles from the German border. He lived in these shtetls of Kovno until the age of five.

Life in the shtetls of Kovno was hard, and poverty abounded. At this point in history, Lithuania had become a world-renowned center for Torah learning, and included famous *yeshivas*, rabbinical colleges that established themselves in Telshe, Kovno, and Vilna. They attracted some of the greatest minds worldwide, and early American immigrants even sent their sons back to the "old-country" to learn there. Despite the explosion of the religious Hasidic sects and their mitnagged opponents in his own backyard, my father did not grow up in a religious household. Few did back then; religious adherents made up only a small percentage of the entire Jewish population.

The Jews in these Lithuanian towns lived in meager prosperity and were able to dwell in peace until a wave of pogroms hit the Pale. Pogroms were riots, sanctioned by the local government and often backed by the military. From 1903 to 1906, the local Catholic and gentile populations were encouraged by the Russian Revolution to turn their anger toward the Jews. The anti-Semitic Lithuanians only needed an excuse, no matter how small, to kindle their hatred. They murdered and mutilated their Jewish neighbors. They looted and burned their stores and shops.

Yosef and Lena had seen enough. Fearing for their lives and the lives of their children, they were forced to move. They headed to Kiev in the Ukraine, with the mistaken notion that they could outrun the madness. Unbeknown to them, they had entered the veritable belly of the beast. The Ukraine became the site of the most horrific pogroms ever imagined, with death and destruction unleashed on an unprecedented scale. The wave of pogroms from 1905 to 1906 claimed the lives of over 3100 Jews.

1915: Child Laborer

Despite the oppression of the pogroms, life continued in the Jewish ghettos. Pogroms were vicious punctuations in an otherwise normal, turn-of-the-twentieth-century existence. Around 1900, Kiev was a significant industrial center, and by 1915, it became a major part of the industrial revolution. To help support his impoverished family, my father had to abandon his childhood and find a full-time job. And so, at the end of the fourth grade, he started working in a garment factory in Kiev. He was ten years old.

The treatment of children in these factories was often cruel and unusual, and the children's safety was generally neglected in classical

Dickensian fashion. These children worked for factory owners and bosses who verbally abused and beat them. My father worked for a typical factory boss who assaulted the boys. My father and the other child co-workers received regular thrashings. He and his friends became resentful of their horrible boss and they started smoking as a way to relieve the pressures of their existence. Although formally banned in 1922, child labor was widespread in the Soviet Union, mostly in the form of mandatory, unpaid work by schoolchildren on Saturdays and holidays.

1917: Child Soldier

In 1917, my father was pulled from the factory and drafted into the army of Czar Nicholas II to fight against the Bolsheviks in the Russian Revolution. If I follow the time line correctly, he would have been no older than twelve, and it was even common for younger boys to be conscripted into the Imperial Military. Thankfully he only served for a short period; in February of that year, the Russian royal family was imprisoned, and in October, Lenin's triumph came quickly. Isaac Shuman, the former czarist child soldier, was now an enemy of the Leninist state. To escape the Bolsheviks, he went into hiding, and for the next two years, he survived within the massive and lush Ukrainian forests.

1920: The Shumans Immigrate

In the early 1920s, most of his family immigrated to the United States. My uncles Sam and Harry, aunt Riva, and my grandparents departed by steamer ship to the port of Philadelphia, eventually settling in Norristown, Pennsylvania. According to the history of the Hebrew Immigrant Aid Society (HIAS) of Pennsylvania:

> in 1882, a group of distinguished members of Philadelphia's Jewish community, led by Louis Levy, formed the Association for the Protection of Jewish Immigrants to assist the influx of Eastern European Jews coming to the Philadelphia region. The

increase in Jewish migration resulted from a wave of pogroms (attacks against Jewish communities that destroyed homes and lives) in Russia that left 100,000 Jews homeless. The persecution of Jews continued unabated, compelling nearly 10,000 Jews to seek refuge in the U.S.[2]

It is more than likely that this group aided my family, and it explains how its members came to reside in Norristown. For reasons unknown, my uncle Leo did not join the family in their move to the United States, instead heading to the port of Havana, Cuba. In the spring of 1921 at the age of sixteen, Isaac was the last one to depart. According to ship records, my father traveled on the White Star Line's *Adriatic II*, one of the four big ships in their service.

The other three ships of White Star Line were the *Celtic*, the *Cedric*, and the *Baltic*. These ships carried massive numbers of passengers: four hundred passengers in first and second-class and over two thousand in third class. In addition, the ships had extremely large storage capacities and were able to carry up to seventeen thousand tons of general cargo. With scant funds, my father traveled in third class, living in the dormitory for single males located in the aft of the ship. The White Star Company was also known for its luxurious Olympic class liners: the *Olympic*, the *Britannic*, and the infamous *Titanic*.

My father's ship was bound for New York, and like all trans-Atlantic journeys, it took many months. At the end of the voyage, the large steamer pulled into the mouth of the Hudson River. My father and all of the passengers went topside, huddling on the ship's deck. Everyone excitedly stood against the ship's railings. Some people were speechless, while others cheered, waving to any passersby they could see. The lucky ones hoped to catch a glimpse of an awaiting relative. My father was treated to sights he had only heard of or seen in pictures: great rising

---

2 HIAS Pennsylvania. Opening Doors for New Americans since 1882. "Our History." Accessed June 21, 2016 *http://hiaspa.org/about-us/legacy*

skyscrapers that crowded the financial district and the Statue of Liberty. They left him breathless.

The steamship my father Isaac sailed on from Russia to New York: The White Star Line's *Adriatic II* arriving in New York Harbor, ca. 1921

Slowly, the great ship pulled into a slip at the New York Harbor. It was a busy place with ocean-going steamers arriving about every twenty minutes. Amidst the chaos, my father reported to an immigration officer who was standing on the dock at the foot of the gangway.

The new arrivals were required to give their personal details: age, height, weight, profession, and country of origin. My father's passport was Russian, and he reported without hesitation that he was from Russia, thinking nothing of it. At once he was told that the Russian quota had been closed. Crestfallen, he and his other countrymen were sequestered with their belongings and luggage and then given over to the immigration authorities and transported to Ellis Island, where they were held indefinitely. With entry into the United States denied, my father contacted his brother Leo, who immediately arranged for him to obtain a Cuban visa, and the two brothers were reunited in Havana.

Three

1925: My Mother Plans a Trip to Cuba

After WWI, the 1921 Russo-Polish War erupted. Russia was pushed back, and Poland no longer served as its vassal state. Now the little northeastern shtetl of Dąbrowa Białostocka was firmly within Polish borders. To celebrate their independence, the Jew-hating Poles committed 130 pogroms throughout the land. Due to the constant looting and rioting, the majority of Jews fled. According to Michael Niven's book on Dąbrowa Białostocka, "The 1921 census recorded 1218 Jews in Dąbrowa out of a total of 3014 with about 300 Jewish families. Passage of America's first immigration effectively closed 'the golden door' and, as a result, emigration during the 1920s and 1930s was much reduced and became oriented toward South America, Cuba and Palestine with only about 10% of Polish Jews now going to the United States." [3]

My mother's older brother Chaim had a number of friends from Dąbrowa who had moved to Mexico and became financially successful. They convinced Chaim to join them, but upon his arrival in Mexico, he discovered that the cost of a landing visa would leave him totally penniless. He immediately decided to proceed to his next port of call, Havana, Cuba. Chaim arrived in Havana without money, friends, or family and not knowing a word of Spanish. It was a tremendous challenge that he was eager to overcome one step at a time. And so, with tremendous faith and an entrepreneurial spirit, he rented an ice-cream pushcart. Less

---

3 Nevins, Michael A. *Dubrowa: Memorial to a Shtetl.* Spring Valley, New York: 2000. Accessed June 21, 2016. http://www.jewishgen.org/Yizkor/Dabrowa_Bialostocka/dab000.html

than twenty-four hours after his arrival in Cuba, my uncle Chaim was selling ice cream on the sunny streets of Havana.

Chaim always kept in touch with the family he left behind in Poland, and my mother Sara became his most avid correspondent. When she wrote him about her inability to continue her education, Chaim excitedly invited her to Cuba. Education in Cuba was totally free, and Chaim promised to help her out with everything else. She would move into his apartment and learn Spanish in night school. Excited and nervous, thirteen-year-old Sara made a decision. She would leave her beloved hometown of Dąbrowa Białostocka, Poland for Havana, Cuba.

1925: The Voyage

After WWI, Poland was free from the crossfire between Germany and Russia. The "newly" independent Poland allowed many Jews the ability to leave for good. Grodno and Bialystok were two regions most noted for the migration, especially of young women, my mother included. In the winter of 1925, my mother, accompanied by her parents, hired a horse-drawn carriage to take them from their tiny town of Dąbrowa Białostocka to the city of Bialystok. The 44-mile trip lasted the better part of a morning. They arrived at the city's railway depot where they boarded a train for the nearly 240-mile trip to the port of Gdansk in the Baltic Sea. From there, my mother hugged, kissed and waved goodbye to her parents. She boarded a steamship; the SS Minnekahda II bound for Cuba. Steamers were common for long-distance travel in the early twentieth century and my mother's three-month voyage was no exception. Along the way, the ship exchanged passengers and loaded supplies at ports in northern France; Vigo, Spain; Lisbon, Portugal; and the Azores. For the first time, my mother saw a world much bigger than her shtetl. As a young, lonely girl on a long voyage, Sara found other girls her age who were in the same situation, girls who had left their families in search of a safer life. On the long voyage, these youthful solitary travelers quickly befriended each other. In Yiddish, they called themselves *shif-shvesters*, "ship-sisters," and they maintained these friendships their entire lives. It was the early spring of 1925 when their ship finally arrived in the port of Havana, Cuba.

The steamship my mother Sara sailed on from
Gdansk, Poland to Havana, Cuba:
The SS Minnekahda II, ca. 1925

What Sara didn't know was that during her voyage, Chaim married, and his wife Pola (née Grossman) was now pregnant. Upon my mother's arrival to Cuba, three long months after leaving Poland, she learned of Chaim's new life. She was dejected. Chaim was no longer able to help her, and the plan to continue her education was shattered. She rented a small apartment with some of her *shif-shvesters*, found a day job in a shirt factory that belonged to an American Jew (whom I only knew as Mr. Shapiro), and went to night school to learn Spanish. My mother was already fluent in Polish, Russian, Hebrew, Yiddish, and German, and since she excelled in languages, she graduated with outstanding grades and spoke Spanish like a native Cuban. No one in Cuba could believe she was a *Polaco*, a nickname the Cubans used for the immigrant Jews from Eastern Europe.

In researching this early chapter in my mother's life, I located the shirt factory in an area known as Guanabacoa. Guanabacoa is located on a hill surrounded by rivers, three miles to the west of central Havana. The area claims a rich history, originally inhabited (as was the entire island) by the indigenous Taíno, Ciboney (a western Taíno group) and Gaunahatabey tribes. These hunter/gatherer people lived on Cuban soil for millennia, a fact corroborated by archeological findings. Nearly two hundred thousand natives inhabited Cuba before colonization by the Spanish Conquistadors. The Spaniards forced the natives to live on reservations. Guanabacoa was one of those reservations. Many of these Indo-Cubans died as a direct result of the physical brutality inflicted by the Spaniards and from diseases such as measles and smallpox. Unknowingly, the natives offered their own vengeance by introducing the smoking of tobacco and most probably syphilis. The Spanish Conquistadors intermarried with the Indo-Cubans. Their children, a mixture of native and European ancestry, were called *mestizos*, a term still used today in Cuba and parts of South America.

In the early twentieth century, Guanabacoa was the place to go if you were an entrepreneurial Jewish textile manufacturer. In the late 1920s, Samuel Epstein, owner of Aetna Knitted Fabrics from New York's lower east side, rented facilities in Guanabacoa. There, he created the Cuban arm of his garment business, producing underwear, shawls, and scarves under the famous brand name *Sedanita*, literally "little silk." He imported $75,000 of equipment and employed two hundred workers. In the 1930s, he sold Sedanita, and the factory was relocated a few miles southwest of Havana, in San Jose de las Lajas. Charles Shapiro, who used it to expand his own knitting and dying company, soon bought the now vacant building in Guanabacoa. Finally, I discovered the identity of the enigmatic shirt-factory owner known only to me as Mr. Shapiro, my mother's first employer.

Two Jewish cemeteries that sit next to each other attest to the strong Jewish presence in Guanabacoa. First founded in 1906, the *Centro Macabeo de Cuba* was used by the Eastern European Ashkenazi community. Its construction was completed in 1910 with the aid of American funds, which explains the English phrase *United Hebrew Congregation* on its frontispiece. The other graveyard is the *Cementerio Sefardí*, which served the Western European and North African Sephardic community of Havana.

The Centro Macabeo de Cuba
Ashkenazi Cemetery,
The Ashkenazi Cemetery in
Guanabacoa, Cuba

Cementerio Israelita,
The Sephardic Cemetery in
Guanabacoa, Cuba

In 2013, it was discovered that the many of the graves were vandalized. Marble headstones were broken and reassembled. Graves were disturbed, the bodies dug up, and the bones removed. There has been much speculation regarding this widespread desecration. The first is the popular suspicion that Jews bury their dead with jewelry. However, the Castro government educated its population against this myth.

The second is that with Raúl Castro's new leadership, Cuba has marginally "opened up," allowing some private enterprise such as restaurants and the sale of land. A widening construction industry came with new landownership. Marble is a commodity of high-market value in construction and could be appropriated from the gravesites for construction purposes. The challenge with this explanation is that none of the damaged marble was missing.

The third possibility is the eeriest and, unfortunately, the most plausible. The town of Guanabacoa is well known for its large following of the white-magic based religion, Santería. It is a uniquely Caribbean belief that blends the West African elements of Nigeria with Catholic motifs. Less well known is its counterpart, a religion that blends the Congo and Catholic, known as *Palo Mayombe*, *Regla de Palo Monte*, or simply *Palo Monte*. It is said to be the world's most powerful and feared form of black magic, eclipsing Voodoo, Satanism, and certain forms of Paganism.

One of the rituals of Palo Monte requires the use of bones from non-baptized people, the main sources of which are supposedly from Jewish graveyards. The *palero*, a Palo Monte priest, requires these bones since they are the only ones capable of warding off the evil eye. With the influx of Cuban immigrants over the decades, the practice was brought to the United States. Recently, it has been reported that in New Jersey, followers of Palo Monte have paid up to $5,000 for a nonbaptized skull. Many members of Santería avoid being associated with Palo Monte.

Four

1930: A Marriage Made in Havana

My mother was eighteen and ready for marriage. In those days, dating was done in groups. You never asked a girl out on a casual date. Instead, parties were held at different homes, and everyone was always invited. As our parents often told us, Jewish girls were to be respected, and marriage was the definitive goal. It was a refined way of saying no premarital hanky-panky and that one-on-one dating was for those who were serious about getting married. The young Jewish social circles flourished in that beautiful, cosmopolitan Caribbean city of Havana. Sara quickly became part of it, and soon the dating scene led her to meet a well-to-do Russian bachelor, who would become my uncle, Leo Chuman. Leo changed the spelling of his last name from Shuman to Chuman because Cubans had difficultly pronouncing *sh*; the *ch* was easier on the Latin tongue. Like my father, Leo only had a fourth-grade education, but despite this, he was a self-made man.

Since my mother was looking for a man with marital interests, Leo introduced her to his brother, Isaac Shuman. After a few dates, eighteen-year-old Sara and twenty-five-year old Isaac married in 1930. Their wedding was held at Chevet Achim. Built in 1914, it was Cuba's oldest synagogue. The newlyweds settled in Havana, and Isaac went to work for his brother Leo.

Leo first owned a haberdashery in the middle-class Marianao neighborhood. After selling it, he opened a men's clothing store only four blocks from my parent's home. He named it after himself: *La Casa Lazaro*, Lazer's House. With an in-house tailor, he sold both premade suits and bolts of fabric for custom-made suits. He loved to play the Cuban lottery, and in 1940, he won $10,000 ($166,000 in today's currency). It was his ticket to leave Cuba and move to the United States. Uncle Leo applied for a green card at the American Embassy, and they issued it in a very short time. He went straight to New York and opened a business selling large stocks of material for clothing. Leo had connections with Jewish merchants in Latin America, and he became highly successful selling his goods in both North and South America.

After working for Leo, my father soon decided to open his own business. My parents opened a ladies' garment factory in a Spanish colonial building converted into rentable units for both commercial and residential use. It was in the Old Havana section of town, and they quickly became highly successful. One room was dedicated to the manufacture of the latest American style dresses, and the other was the storefront for selling them. My father traveled to the New York fashion shows twice a year and brought back coffee-table-style fashion books.

My mother had the ability to simply look at the pictures in these books, and with her photographic memory, she could then cut fabric for the hundreds of new dress patterns that came out each year. Maria

A page from a fashion book
ca.1940 that my father
brought back from one
of his many trips to the
New York Fashion Shows

Josepha was their seamstress and my parent's only employee. She sewed the pieces together as my mother gave them to her; theirs was no sweatshop by any means.

The flight manifest from one of my father's trips
to the United States on Pan Am flight #442

Five

1932: My Sister, Anita

In 1932, my sister, Ana, was born. Nicknamed Anita, she had tremendous energy and spirit. A natural-born leader, Anita was popular in her circle of Jewish friends. She went to *Yavneh*, the first Jewish elementary school in Havana. From there, she attended the *Instituto del Vedado*, a public high school in the upper class Vedado section of Havana. Anita wanted to go to medical school, but our mother forbade it; medicine required one to go out at night and see patients and for a young lady, our mother deemed it an inappropriate profession. They argued about this a lot, but, in the end, mama won out. Anita was devastated. In those days, girls were meant to be housewives. Despite our mother's insistence on a domestic lifestyle, Anita went to pharmacy school at the University of Havana. After two years, the Castro government curtailed her studies and she was forced to flee Cuba. Years later, still yearning for a higher education, she received her masters in social work from Brooklyn City College at the age of fifty-two.

1939: My Birth

On October 5, 1939, I was born in a second-story apartment in the downtown business district of Havana, at 601 Neptuno Street. I was named Joseph after my late paternal grandfather, but Cuban law required an official Spanish name so my official Cuban birth certificate listed me as José. In Cuba, I was called José or Pepe, the affectionate Spanish nickname for José,. Like most Jews who have a Hebrew name, a name local to the country they live in and perhaps a nickname, I could be called Joseph, *Yosef,* José, Pepe, or Joe as friends and family in the United States knew me. As a child, it didn't matter what I was called. Growing up in Cuba in the 1940's, nothing really bothered me, especially something as trivial as a name. Life in Cuba was like living in a fantasy. I felt as if I grew up on a magical island where palm trees abounded and a trip to gorgeous beaches of pure white sand was only a block from our summer home.

Elementary School el Yiddish

Yavneh, the elementary school Anita attended closed, so I went to *El Plantel del Centro Israelita de Cuba,* established by local Jewish socialist groups. In the morning, we learned conversational Yiddish, and in the afternoon, general studies, including English as a language, which started in fourth grade.

Left to right: Anita and me, ages 10 and 3. Me in a sailors suit, age 4. In the park with my mother Sara age 35, me on a bike age 7, and Anita, age 14

In today's Jewish schools, Hebrew is taught, but, back then, we learned Yiddish. Hebrew was considered a foreign language because Israel was not yet a state. However, my mother felt it very important that I learned basic elementary Hebrew, and she arranged for her sister, my *tante* Freidel to teach it to me. My parents had high academic expectations of their only son. I remember the pressures they placed on me, even as a young boy. In the first grade, my teacher gave us a math test, but I didn't understand the questions. It was the only failing grade I ever received. I cried and told the teacher that if I failed, my mother threatened to send me to the dog pound. It was obviously a complete fabrication on my mother's part, but, to a six-year-old boy, it was as real as could be.

That early pressure resulted in my success as a straight-*A* student. In fact, when I completed the sixth grade, there was a formal graduation ceremony. I was valedictorian and gave the graduation speech. Amazingly, I didn't stutter (a problem I developed as a young child), but it was because I practiced quite a bit. I was awarded a solid eighteen-karat gold medal that I proudly wore around my neck and that Castro stole from me before I left Cuba six years later.

My sixth-grade graduation, age 12. On the far right is Señor Elias Eliovitch, our principle of Jewish studies. I am the second student from the right.

Six

Kashrut: Cuban Style

Life was easygoing in this tropical Eden. I remember walking with my mother to a kosher bakery, Café Lily. They baked traditional Jewish breads, sweet cookies, and cakes. As good as those pastries were, to me, they were too Eastern European, and not as appealing as the treats made by the island locals. My father and I preferred the *treif* (non-kosher) Cuban bakery two blocks from our apartment. They made round bread with a peaked sugary top called pan de Gloria.

For breakfast, I spread butter over my pan de Gloria and together with the requisite cup of strong Cuban coffee, I was in heaven. They also made traditional Cuban sandwiches of *chazer* (pork or ham) that my father and I brought home. When we ate chazer and treif in the house, my mother always made a fuss, making sure to cover the table with newspaper. I think she did it more for show. My father and I enjoyed these meals with beer or Malta, a popular nonfermented beer that was also known as *la cerveza de los hijos*, children's beer.

We even had a kosher restaurant that opened in the forties in the old section of Havana. The restaurant was called Moishe Pipik. It was a hotspot for strictly kosher tourists and a familiar haven for the locals. I remember the owner only by her first name, Reizel. They served typical Eastern European Jewish fare like matzo ball soup and various chicken dishes. My friends and I loved it.

Oddly enough, when it came to *kashrut* (keeping kosher), I found the Cuban Jewish community (then twenty thousand people) to be peculiar and interesting. They kept kosher homes as best they could but

A business card and promotional postcard for the kosher
restaurant Moishe Pipik, Havana, Cuba, 1955

ate at any restaurant, kosher or not. I guess you could say the community was traditional, holding on to some of the ways they were raised under Eastern European Orthodoxy, yet reaching out for a comfortable life in Cuba. I don't remember anyone ever tagging us with a religious label, but today we would probably be considered Conservative or Reform. In those days, religion was not a priority. For those who survived the pogroms or escaped the Nazi terror and their concentration camps or, like my father, the horrors of war under the Imperial Russian czar, just being alive and functioning was enough.

Most of the Jews who arrived in Cuba were from the European socialist movement. They were traditional, meaning they kept the major holidays, but Shabbos was not strictly observed. On Friday night they lit candles, and then went to the movies. My mother was from a *frum* (orthodox) family, but in Cuba it was extremely difficult to keep a strictly observant orthodox life, so she did what she could. I remember that Saturdays were special, but for a different reason. Every Saturday afternoon, my sister Anita took me to F. W. Woolworth, which we fondly called the "*Tencent*". We sat at the lunch counter and ordered a club sandwich of *ensalada de pollo* (chicken salad) or *de bonito* (tuna) with a milkshake or fountain soda. On special occasions, I was treated to a plate of flan, flanked by two scoops of ice cream. It was artery-clogging in high gear, but we didn't know any better. We just ate and enjoyed.

Keeping kosher in the home meant buying kosher meat and chicken, and for that, everyone went to Yankele the butcher. They called him "*Yankele the Ganef*" because he charged twice the price of nonkosher meat. Calling anyone a *ganef* (thief) was a serious accusation, but whenever I think about Yankele, it makes me chuckle. Eventually, his steep prices dropped as they gave way to healthy competition from Chervony's Butcher Shop. Our community was small, and I remember going to school with Isaac Chervony, the butcher's nephew.

Seven

Memories of My Father

Papa, as my sister and I called him, was a no-nonsense guy who, ironically, had a great sense of humor. He was also a nervous person. With lunch being the traditional big meal in Cuba, we always sat as a family for the midday feast. If we misbehaved, he stood up and left the house, slamming the door on the way out. In those days, if a child misbehaved, their parents gave them a healthy *zetz* (Yiddish for a "smack"). Not my father. He was never physically abusive and never laid a hand on me except one time. My parents came home from the store at lunchtime and at the end of the day. Because of the heat and humidity, my dad showered twice a day and expected the bathroom to be empty when he came home. The problem was that I had a funny habit of using the bathroom right at that time. I'm not sure why I did it, but nature always seemed to call at just the wrong moment. One day he lost it and gave me a *zetz*. It was so shocking that I was instantly cured and never occupied the *baño* during dad's arrival.

My father was always well dressed. On special occasions, such as the Sunday night theater, he wore a traditional Cuban suit made of fine Irish linen that was stiffly starched at the Chinese cleaners. If you wanted to look good in a linen suit, you had to stand because the material wrinkled instantly after sitting. During the week, he wore dress pants and a *guaya-bera*, the customary Latin button-down shirt adorned with several pockets and vertical pleats between them. My father was prematurely bald and used pomades like Brylcreem and Vitalis to slick back his thinning black hair.

His eyes were light-sensitive, and he always wore dark sunglasses, even in the movie theater. My father usually fell asleep at the movies (a gift I inherited as well) and snored, earning him a shot in the ribs from my mother. On Sunday mornings, he always took me to a park where we rented bikes. It was there that he taught me to ride a bike. He was also a nervous wreck, always complaining of stomach ailments. He was the kind of guy who broke promises all the time, offering to take me to the movie matinee and cancelling at the last minute because of a stomachache.

He saw his gastroenterologist several times a month and was told he had "dispepsia nerviosa," a nervous stomach. By today's standards, it would probably be diagnosed as an ulcer of psychogenic origin. He drank Phillips' Milk of Magnesia, which, to him, was a cure-all. He also had two vices: nicotine and caffeine. He smoked two packs of Regalias el Cuño (The Royal Stamp) cigarettes a day. In addition to the heavy nicotine from chain smoking, he drank five to ten *cortaditos*, demitasse-sized cups of intensely strong black Cuban coffee at the corner shop for three cents apiece. I'm sure that didn't help his problem.

An ad for my father's favorite
brand of cigarettes ca. 1945.
(The ad reads: **The Royal Stamp**
Satisfies! Buy them here!)

The Garment Business

As a wholesaler, my father sold the latest American style dresses through-out the island. Almost every successful merchant in Cuba traveled by car, but my father was reluctant to buy a car because he didn't have the cour-age to drive it, (like I said, he was a nervous man). So at the beginning of his traveling salesman career, he made his rounds by bus.

The bus rides were long and hot, and the driver made frequent rest stops. On one trip, my father went to a roadside bathroom and found a wallet lying on the bathroom floor. In it was over $2000, and in those times, the strong Cuban economy made the Cuban peso equal to the US dollar, one to one. My father was so honest that he brought the wallet home, found the owner's ID, called him, and returned the wallet. The man tipped him $20 as thanks. I witnessed the entire episode, and it had a profound effect on me. To this day, I have emulated his honest ways completely. For that alone, I thank him.

Eight

1942 and the Modern Age: Escalators, Air Conditioning, and Packards

In 1942, Sears opened its first international store in Havana. It was the first local retail establishment to boast central air conditioning and escalators. In a country where we slept with open windows and a sheet over your entire body as the only line of defense against hordes of aggressive mosquitoes, air conditioning was a welcome relief from the subtropical humidity. The escalator was truly a remarkable invention, and we rode it just for the novelty.

1942: The Packard

It really amazes me how I can remember certain details of my childhood so vividly. One recollection in particular was the two cars my father owned. As business improved, he was able to invest in personal transportation and a driver. My father's first car was a 1942 twelve-cylinder light-shaded blue-green Packard with a white roof.

It was a real beast of a car, and it drank gas like one too. After several years, he was no longer enthused with the hefty fuel bill, and in 1946, he sold the Packard. Soon after World War II, the United States began manufacturing cars in earnest. In 1948, my father bought a dark-green Plymouth with a three-shift manual transmission and a slanted rear. He had the entire family memorize the license plate number in case the car was ever stolen. After seventy years, I can still remember that plate number. It was 14592.

My father's first car in Cuba, the
1942 twelve-cylinder Packard

My father's second car in Cuba, a 1948 Plymouth

Candella and Cousin Boris—the Chauffeurs

Even though he had a driver's license, my father was too anxious to maneuver in heavy traffic, and he rarely drove either of the cars himself. He had a chauffeur whose real name I never knew. I just remember that we called him by his nickname, Candella. At some point my father replaced Candella with my first cousin Boris.

Boris was my mother's nephew, the son of Chaim and Pola, who both left Poland in 1919, just after World War I. Like my parents, they met and married in Cuba. Cousin Boris and I shared the fact that we were both Cuban born. Boris worked for a man named Somerstein who had a leather business selling items such as belts and wallets, and he and my father both sold their wares around the island with Boris as their driver. Boris; his mother, Pola; and sister, Ida, applied for permanent-resident visas in the United States. In those days, one of the requirements for US immigration process was to have a chest x-ray taken to rule out tuberculosis. The two ladies were both approved, but Boris's x-ray revealed a shadow. He never had tuberculosis but the State Department required an investigation to rule it out. During the wait, cousin Boris moved in with us.

Nine

1945: Luisa—Mi Segunda Madre (My Second Mother)

Because my parents both worked, they hired a wonderfully warm, live-in housekeeper/nanny named Luisa Negrin. She was known as a *mestiza*, a woman of mixed-racial ancestry. In her case, Luisa was both European and Native Indo-Cuban. She worked for our friends, the Voltianskys. While visiting their home, my mother met Luisa, and they hit it off right away. Soon she came to work for us full time. Luisa was eighteen-years old and came from a poor Catholic family in Los Palos, a tiny town outside Havana.

Luisa was raised on a small farm where her parents grew their own vegetables and raised chickens and pigs that freely wandered the front yard. When I was ten, she took me by train to her family. Since I was a special guest, they had a big meal waiting, minus the pork, as per Luisa's instructions. I remember that despite their home being simple and modest, it was absolutely spotless.

Luisa was a wonderful lady who loved me like one of her own. She became my surrogate mother. She was naïve in the ways of relationships and men. Her charming cousin, a black man named Otilio Garcia, was a foreman at a farm owned by an army major outside Havana. He came to us every Sunday night, and eventually, they became engaged. He always promised marriage, but he secretly had another family. Luisa never married, always holding out for the hope that one day she and Otilio would live happily ever after. That day never came.

1943: Ferrocarril Urbano de la Habana (The Tramways of Havana)

When I was a small child, Luisa filled my days with the many activities available to our Caribbean lifestyle. Whenever we needed to travel anywhere that was too far to walk, we rode the trolley cars of the Havana Electric Railway. This urban transport system was known as *Ferrocarril Urbano de la Habana*, the iron trams of urban Havana. These streetcars rode on tracks, and each car had two thick, long wires protruding from its roof. These wires ran along a pair of high-voltage overhead lines that powered the system. These railway tracks and high wires crisscrossed all over Havana.

Ferrocarril Urbano de la Habana, the Havana streetcars I rode as a child.
Tram 591, photographed on *Calle Neptuno*, ca. 1949

On a bright sunny day when I was four years old, Luisa and I were waiting at a tram stop on our way back home from the beach. When a tram pulled in, Luisa held my hand as we boarded the car. The trip usually took about thirty minutes, and when we were halfway home, the sky abruptly turned black, a common occurrence in the Caribbean tropics. Although storms were a part of daily life, this particular storm was massive. Ominous clouds, thick and heavy, were gathering overhead. An initial trickle turned into dense sheets of water. A huge bolt of lightning struck the power lines, followed by a deafening boom. It was a terrifying explosion of sound and fire that shook everyone in the car. The strangers around me were panicking. The driver yelled for everyone to get out of the tram. That incredibly loud blast, mixed with the burst of fire and the people pushing and shoving to get out of that packed trolley car left me in a complete state of shock, so much so that I was unable to speak for several weeks.

Ten

Dr. Alvare—Mi Héroe

There were only two Cubans I can remember who were over six feet tall: Fidel Castro, whom I absolutely despised, and Dr. Emilio de Alvare, whom I completely admired. Dr. Alvare was our family pediatrician. He wore a pencil-thin moustache, rim-wire glasses, and always had a smile. He was unlucky with women, divorcing his first wife, and then falling in love, marrying, and divorcing Lolita, his clinic nurse.

He was really as nice as could be and was very caring with his patients. A house call cost five dollars, and between 1941 and 1942, he made frequent house calls to our apartment. After climbing the two-stories' worth of steps, he developed a coughing fit that produced blood. This was due to the rheumatic heart disease he had contracted years before. He recovered in our living room, and once his coughing subsided, he would see me.

But this time, my mother brought me to his clinic because of my posttraumatic speech loss. I remember sitting on my mother's lap as Dr. Alvare took off his glasses. He did this whenever he needed to emphasize the sincerity of his medical pronouncement. "Don't worry, Mrs. Shuman. Your son has suffered a severe psychological shock. He will soon be fine, and his speech will return." If Dr. Alvare said it, it was gospel.

My mother thanked him, and we went back home. My parents were still concerned, especially my mother, who worried about everything to the point where the psychological stress turned into physical illness. (She suffered with constant migraines and had seven heart attacks over the course of her life.)

True to his word, Dr. Alvare's pronouncement came to fruition, and after a month, my ability to speak slowly returned. With it came a pronounced stutter. The stuttering worsened in unsecure environments, reminiscent of that fateful trolley fire. I tried correcting the problem by attending speech therapy. My first therapist was the famous Cuban radio voice actor, Juan Jose Castellanos. Those sessions didn't help much, and the stutter remained, essentially untreated.

It was never a real hindrance, but it wasn't the smoothest way to speak. That changed in 1971, when I began my medical residency at the University of Pittsburgh. They had a speech department, and the therapists wanted to help me. So at the age of thirty-two, these truly wonderful and caring people picked up where Señor Castellanos left off. The most effective exercise I learned was to consciously start my sentences with words I didn't have problems with. I was taught to substitute difficult words with their synonyms. I practiced constantly, and it took years to improve.

As for the trams, I remember that they were permanently removed in the 1950s, including the tracks. The streets where they ran were rebuilt and freshly paved. Autobuses Modernos S. A. substituted the trams. These were brand-new white buses made by Leyland in England. The people renamed these modern buses *las enfermeras,* (the nurses), because

The *Autobuses Modernos S. A.*, made by the
British company, Leyland ca. 1950

they were painted entirely in white. They were all manual transmission and, being British-made, were notoriously difficult to maneuver.

Therefore, Havana needed a second bus company. The *Cooperativa de Omnibus Aliados,* (COA) had sleek buses made by General Motors, and the majority of them had automatic transmissions.

Eleven

1944: Titi and Potri

My father often brought me gifts when he arrived home in the evenings. One day, he brought two chickens that I was to look after as pets. As any excited five-year old would do, I named them Titi and Potri after the sounds they made. I kept them on one of the balconies. At that time of year, hurricane season was upon us, and we were struck by the 1944 hurricane that invaded Havana. As that storm raged, I called their names through the closed balcony doors. When I heard their sounds, I knew they were okay. Eventually the storm passed. My pet chickens survived the great hurricane of 1944.

Over the next several months, part of my daily routine included making sure Titi and Potri were well and had enough to eat. One day, I opened the balcony door to visit with my pets, but they were nowhere to be found. I was dumbstruck. When I asked Luisa what had happened to them, she told me they flew away. That day, we ate chicken for lunch, and like any naïve, trusting child, I thought nothing of it. A few months later my sister told me that we had eaten my pets. I cried, not only because of their demise but because Luisa had lied to me. This went against everything my father had taught me. Titi and Potri may have survived a hurricane but not Luisa's butchering. There are just some things that children never forget and for me this was one of them.

Each week, Luisa's one day off was Sunday. She would go to church, and then get ready for her boyfriend Otilio to visit her in the evening. With Luisa unavailable, Sunday was my mother's turn in the kitchen. She was a terrific cook and would make all sorts of traditional Jewish dishes.

She would make *tzimmes,* a sweet stew common to Eastern Europe. Her *tzimmes* would include diced carrots, prunes and honey. It was delicious and had the added benefit of gentle gastrointestinal persuasion. She would go to the local fish market, buy the daily catch of cod and pike and grind the fish in a meat grinder. Spices were added to the ground fish, and it was formed into a loaf and boiled with carrots and onions. Mama also made kugels and cheese blintzes. These were tastes of the old country and it seemed out of place in the Caribbean, but to me, these old-fashioned dishes were comforting and familiar.

I also remember the problems we had with insects. Luisa kept our apartment extremely neat and clean, but even the most immaculate homes in Cuba had cockroach visits. These were monstrous, flying things, two to three inches in length and were endemic to our hot, tropical climate. Another problem was the *chinches,* commonly known as bedbugs and they were prevalent in most homes. Exterminators came to the house spraying DDT out of big metal cans. It definitely killed the bedbugs, for a period of time anyway. When they returned, Luisa killed them by spritzing the mattresses with boiling water, and then laying them on the balcony to dry. Luisa's method kept us bedbug free for a week, but they always returned. This lasted throughout my childhood.

Another serious issue we dealt with in Cuba was the drinking water. Back then (as it is today) Cuban tap water was full of bacteria, parasites, and other tropical pathogens. The most common diseases from this water were cholera, typhoid and hepatitis. So for most Cubans, there were two options: boil the water at home or hire a potable-water delivery service. My mother was not about to boil water on a daily basis or bother Luisa with the task, so we had our water delivered. The ingenuity of the time was not the bottled water but how it was delivered. Without phone service or Internet, the 1940s method was a string and paper. The water delivery truck drove around the neighborhood every week. If we needed water, my mother attached a piece of newspaper to a string and tied it to the balcony. When the driver saw this sign, he delivered the water and removed the empty bottles. It was that simple.

1944: Hurricanes and Hot Chocolate

To a six-year-old boy, the hurricane of 1944 was memorable. On October 12, it became the third major hurricane of the season. It slowly developed over the southern Caribbean Sea and, after five days, struck Cuba full-force with winds of 160 miles per hour. On October 17, a province known as Pinar del Rio, on the very west coast of Cuba, was hit hardest. Havana is located at the northwestern portion of the island, and we were hit with the hurricane as it moved northward and eastward to the Florida coast. We lived five blocks from the ocean in a Spanish colonial from Malecon Avenue, a road that spanned the seashore.

To prevent our windows from being destroyed, my mother and Luisa fortified them with heavy tape. When the tempest arrived, my sister told me to look out the window at the ocean. I looked out through a gap in the tape; the waves were thirty feet high, and they crashed over the fifteen-foot concrete levee walls, flooding the blocks ahead of us. In those days, homes were built on solid foundations, and roofs were made of concrete, so they never flew away. I watched as neon signs from local businesses broke away from their posts, their shattered colored glass appearing like beautiful crystals of shrapnel. My father was away from home on one of his business trips to New York, so I was alone with my mother, Anita, and Luisa. I actually looked forward to hurricane season and the storms themselves, because Luisa always made me hot chocolate.

The Havana weather bureau announced on the CMQ radio station that we could sleep well that night since the storm was traveling away from Cuba and toward the United States.

At two in the morning, the storm traveled north to Florida. The harbor in Havana was littered with sunken and broken ships. Pieces of people's lives were scattered everywhere. As the storm died down, my mother became consumed with checking in on my father's shop to see if it was still intact. She walked barefoot through the flooded streets to the old section of Havana. It took over two hours, but she was determined.

The radio reported that approximately three hundred people had died, most in Pinar del Rio and several other rural areas. By the time the category-four storm had ended in the northeastern portion of the United States, over $40 billion in damage had occurred.

Twelve

1947: Quinceañeras and Our Lady of Charity

In 1947, my sister celebrated her fifteenth birthday, and as was the custom throughout Latin America and the Caribbean, a *Quinceañera* was a must. A girl's fifteenth birthday calls for a grand celebration, as it signifies her transition from childhood to womanhood. I found this interesting, since her bat mitzvah celebrated the same at age twelve. However, these occasions are celebrated for different reasons. In the Jewish liturgy, a bat mitzvah (and bar mitzvah for boys) marks a transition into adulthood for reasons of maturity and with it the acceptance of the laws of Moses. In the Latin tradition, girls were prepared to either be married by the age of fifteen or become nuns. If you knew Anita and my mother, this was absolutely hilarious: Anita was no nun, and marriage at fifteen was never going to happen if my mother had anything to do with it. So it was celebrated because the Latin tradition called for it and "when in Rome…"

I recall Anita wearing a beautiful long, pink gown that my mother had personally designed and created in their clothing store. The party was held at Union Sionista de Cuba, the Zionist Union of Cuba, a familiar haunt for the weekly Friday night meetings of my sister's chapter of *Hashomer Hatzair*, the international movement of Zionist youth. So like everything else in that blender of cultures that was so iconic of Cuba, my sister had her traditionally Latin American fifteenth birthday celebration in a distinctly political Jewish building.

Union Sionista de Cuba, the Zionist Union of
Cuba where my sister had her *Quinceañera*

Another melding of traditions was the Afro-Cuban fusion of
Catholicism and ancient African Yoruba beliefs, spawning the religion
known as Santería. On the whole, Cubans were Catholic, and, typical
of Latin Catholics, they relied heavily on the worship and celebration
of their saints. Every September 8, Our Lady of Charity, *La Virgen de la
Caridad de Cobre*, the patroness saint of Cuba was worshipped throughout the island. (Coincidentally, September 8 was also the birthday of my
friend Elias Vilkas and we made fun of him for that.) In the Santería
religion, Our Lady of Charity is syncretized with Ochún, a deity originat-
ing in Yorubaland, Nigeria. This union allowed people from different
religious backgrounds to share in a common belief. I remember masses
of people walking in long, disorganized columns in downtown Havana.
Many traveled to the city of Santiago de Cuba, the "second capital" of
Cuba where the Virgin's National Sanctuary is located.

There was also a legend that every year on December 4, the blood
of children was needed for worshipping Changó, the warrior saint who
was syncretized with Santa Barbara. Rumors floated about that On
December 4, children who walked alone in the city could be kidnapped
and sacrificed. Of course it was utter nonsense, but my mother bought
into the blood libel and was uneasy to let me go anywhere by myself on
that day.

These many saint worshiping street processions never made much of an impression on me. It was common pageantry that occurred throughout the year, both alien, yet familiar. What did make an impression was a trip I took with Louisa at the age of eight. Louisa had two sisters, Lorenza and Minerva. One day, she took me to visit Lorenza and her family. When I entered the house, there, in front of me, was an enormous shrine to Our Lady of Charity. It was actually set up in their living room, like you or I would have a coffee table. At the center was a statue of the virgin surrounded by flowers and gifts. I was dumbstruck; what the heck was this? The virgin was no longer an odd curiosity. It was personal. It actually belonged to someone I knew, and it scared me. My gaze went from this elaborate homemade shrine to Lorenza's husband.

My knowledge of Cuban saint worship was minimal; after all, what did Jewish kids know about Afro-Cuban deities? From what I heard, this statue probably required the blood sacrifice of a child. Was I the latest unwilling lamb? From the stories my mother told me, people who followed Santería used this shrine, and one of their religious rites was the slaughter of animals. I quickly turned pale. Louisa could sense my unease. She took my hand and we made a quick exit out of the living room to the kitchen. Louisa took me aside and explained the meaning of the statue and the importance of this national idol. I was relieved when she informed me that there would be no child sacrifices. Once I calmed down, Luisa offered me lunch, but my appetite had vanished.

There were other patron saints celebrated in Cuba. April 17 was the day reserved for San Lázaro (Saint Lazarus). My uncle Leo happened to share his name because in Spanish, Leo is short for Lázaro, and every April 17 we told him it was "his day". San Lázaro was purported to have extreme healing powers. The big San Lázaro celebration was held in El Rincón, about 15 miles south of Havana. Some worshippers would crawl on their knees for miles, and on their arrival at the shrine in Rincon, ask for his healing powers. Foregoing sore knees, Louisa traveled to the shrine by bus. In Santería, San Lázaro is compared to Babalú Aye, a Yoruba deity, who was also invoked to cure health problems.

This reminds me of other Santería stories. I recall that in Guanabacoa, a Santería priest known as a *Babalawo*, lived there. In the African Yoruba language, Babalawo literally means 'father of the mysteries'. People saw this holy man for advice on opening businesses, taking trips, love interests, and other daily issues. He shook sacred palm nuts between cupped hands and threw them on a divining tray. He read the configurations, and then pronounced his findings.

Several years ago, I had a patient who became very ill. Before he came to see me, he made a promise to Santa Barbara following a common Cuban custom: he would wear white clothing for a full year if he were healed. After a complete recovery, he made a visit to my office, and sure enough, from shoes to shirt, he was dressed in white. So if you see a Cuban completely dressed in white, it is likely he is keeping a promise to the virgin for something important.

Thirteen

1949: The Infamous Guanabo Beach "Chicken in the Freezer"

Candella would drive us to our beach cabana located on Third Street. It was a block away from Guanabo Beach and the warmer waters of the Caribbean Sea. My parents shared the apartment with my mother's sister Freida and her husband, Boruch. We entered the building from an alleyway. There was a step or two to get into the simple and efficient apartment. A small table with chairs filled most of the dining/living room and a rather small refrigerator/freezer was in the kitchen. There were three bedrooms, perfect for my parents, Anita and I, and Frieda and Boruch.

It was the summer of 1949, and we were all in the cabana apartment. My parents split the rent and living expenses with my aunt and uncle. They even divided the space in the refrigerator/freezer; one half was food we purchased, and the other contained food they purchased. One day, a chicken found its way to the middle of the freezer, and a war had begun over who was the rightful owner. This was a truly Solomonic problem with no solution. My parents moved out and told Boruch that he now had to pay all the expenses, and that summer he was stuck with the bill. The only two sisters remaining in their family didn't speak to each other for ten years because of this overclaimed chicken in the freezer. So today when my kids argue, I tell them, "Let's not start a 'chicken in the freezer.'"

Standing left to right: Boris Yaroshevsky, Sara (Yaroshevsca) Shuman,
Isaac Shuman, Pola (Grossman) Yaroshevsky
Seated left to right: Anita (Shuman) Bondar, Boruch Morduchovitch, Freida
(Yaroshevsca) Morduchovitch, Ida (Yaroshevsky Grossman) Hochrad
I am the boy seated on the platform

Fourteen

1950: Anita's Engagement and Wedding

Our home was either tumultuous or dead silent, depending on the whims of my mother. I've always had the sense that the typical Eastern European parenting in which my mother was raised came from the school of "shoot first and ask questions later." To worsen matters, these Eastern Europeans who were torn from their families and lost many to the Nazi genocide were forever damaged. They held in anger, sadness, depression, and a host of other PTSD-type disorders. For my friends and I who shared parents of this ilk, it was like living with a bipolar bear. Sometimes you experienced the cute and cuddly teddy bear, and sometimes you were subjected to the grizzly.

This parental behavior was typified by a story I recall that involved my sister. In 1950, Anita was busy dating. One rainy night, she went out with a nice young Jewish man named Ricardo Wilkowsky. Her curfew was midnight, but the rain delayed them by an hour. Like a sentry, my mother stood on the balcony with an umbrella waiting for her return. At one o'clock, Mama saw them walking down the street. She moved from the balcony to stand behind the front door. When Anita and Ricardo knocked on the door, Mama yanked it open. She didn't bother to ask why they were late. Mama grizzly bear was incensed, screaming, and yelling at them. I could see that Ricardo was petrified of this four foot ten lunatic. As he ran for the door, Mama threw a chair at him. He never asked Anita out again.

Undaunted, Anita eventually met a nice Jewish man named Raphael (Ralph) Bondar. Ralph was a well-to-do print-shop owner. He was twenty-eight, and Anita was eighteen when they first met. Before WWII, Ralph's family emigrated from their town of Ruzinov, Poland (also the birthplace of the late Israeli prime minister Yitzchak Shamir). Ralph was the oldest of four brothers. His three younger brothers, Moises, David, and Hillel were all married. As the eldest and only single brother, I'm sure Ralph felt pressure to wed. It was all too common in the Jewish-Latin culture.

When Ralph was dating Anita, he would customarily pick her up from our apartment. I remember being ill with the measles, and Ralph brought me a get-well gift. It was a stack of comic books featuring Mickey Mouse, Bugs Bunny, Captain Marvel, Superman, and Batman, all in Spanish. The gift giving became a regular event, and whenever Ralph came by I received my hoard of comic books. I'm sure that paying tribute to the little brother didn't hurt in winning favor with the family, and I loved it when Ralph came to visit.

Anita and Ralph eventually married. At their wedding, I distinctly recall the popular Jewish musician in Havana who we all knew by first name only. Moishe stood about four feet tall with severe kyphoscoliosis, (a deformity of the spine characterized by an abnormal curvature of the vertebral column). His S shaped body was made worse by the fact that he played the violin, holding it between his chin and shoulder. He hired a few Afro-Cuban musicians who played various instruments like bongos, the trumpet, and maracas. Because of his deformity, everyone knew he and his band as "*Jorobeta* and his Cuban Boys" (the Little Hunchback and his Cuban Boys). He was the nicest man, but, unfortunately, people made fun of him. I felt sorry for him and always tried to engage him in conversation. He was incredibly talented and played any type of music, including Cuban, American, Jewish, and a unique fusion that can only be described as Klezmer-Latino. I have no clue what happened to him after Castro's take over.

My sister Anita's engagement party to Ralph Bondar.
Standing L. to R.: David & Rosa Bondar,
Me, Moises & Raquel Bondar, Isaac Perner,
Dr. Emilio de Alvare, Boris, Notary.
Seated L. to R.: Chana Bondar, Ralph
& Anita, Sara & Isaac Shuman

Anita's engagement party: standing from left to
right: Olga Fernandez (our downstairs neighbor),
Anita Hershman, Anita Bondar(Hillel's wife),
Esther Perner, Ida Berger, ???, Sarita Slutzker. Sitting
from left to right: Raquel Arber (Bondar), Esther
Kozolchick, Anita Shuman, ???, Rosa Bondar.

Anita signing the engagement document

Anita and Ralph's wedding

Fifteen

1952: My Bar Mitzvah

I celebrated my bar mitzvah in 1952 at the newly built, modest, concrete building known as Adath Israel Synagogue in the Belen neighborhood in the Old Havana section. Back then, we didn't have pulpit rabbis, so it was run by the *kehilla*, (members of the synagogue). I read the *haftarah*, the weekly portion of the Prophets, taught to me by the same rabbi who performed my bris, Rabbi Mendel Shochet.

He must have been a man in his late forties, and he was one of the few orthodox Jews I knew in Havana. His wife's name was Malka, and she taught Hebrew at Centro Israelita de Cuba. After school, I climbed three flights to their small, sparsely furnished apartment in the Old Havana section. I did this twice a week for one year. Those lessons were an intermingling of three languages: his broken Spanish, a fluent Yiddish, and the cantillations of the Hebrew haftarah and its blessings.

After the ceremony, we made that quintessential Jewish toast to life, the *l'chaim*, and then moved the party to Altman's Restaurant. Altman was a kosher caterer in Havana who didn't really have a formal restaurant. He rented space on the second floor of an old building. In that room, there were long tables set up in a U-shaped fashion, and my family and personal friends were there.

From my understanding, the Adath Israel Synagogue still exists today with a *minyan*, a quorum of ten men, and in this case, all are elderly people. After Rabbi Schochet and his family left Cuba, Rabbi Nissim Gambach, a Sephardic Jew became the mohel. He was the rabbi who performed the bris on both of my nephews, Willy and Milton. Many

My Bar Mitzvah Party at Altman's Catering Room.
Left to right: my father, Isaac Shuman; my mother, Sara Shuman;
Me; my sister Anita (Shuman) Bondar; my brother-in-law, Ralph Bondar

years later, Rabbi Gambach left Cuba and was hired by the Turkish shul on Sixth Avenue in Miami, Florida. He remained the rabbi there until his passing. He was in his late seventies.

Sixteen

1957: Shama, Caribbean Rum, y el Porvenir

In 1957 my father was interested in expanding his business from wholesale manufacturing to include a separate retail outlet. There was a store on the ground floor below his owned by a Polish Jew named Abraham Dick who sold linens such as sheets, towels, and pillowcases. My father told him he wanted to open a retail-clothing store, but he needed a partner who would share the financial burden. Abraham had a brother named Shama who was looking to open a business in Havana, and he introduced Shama to my father.

Shama Dick was a Jewish refugee from Poland who had escaped from a concentration camp, and then fought the Germans with a group of forest partisans. Many who escaped the devastation left by the Nazis were often emotionally destroyed, and Shama Dick was no exception. His wife and two children were murdered in a concentration camp. So, he picked up the pieces and made a new life for himself; he married his niece, the only surviving member of his entire family. When he immigrated to Cuba, Shama lived in Mata in the province of Las Villas, with his wife Shifra and their daughter Celia (Celita). Shama sold *shmatas* (rags) at the Mata store and was wildly successful, but Mata was not known for having any kind of Jewish presence.

Shama and Shifra wanted their daughter to have a Jewish social life, so when Celita turned twelve they moved to Havana. It was 1956 when Shama purchased the first condos available on the island. I was impressed because the condominium, named the FOCSA, was considered an architectural sensation. It was the second largest concrete structure ever built worldwide. The ground floor featured a shopping mall, and my friend Pepe Sinai's father had an upscale toy store there. On the rooftop, the FOCSA even had a rotating restaurant called La Torre, too expensive for us to eat at. Shama paid $17,000 for that condo. With today's inflation, it was the equivalent of just over $150,000, a handsome price at the time.

In the summer of 1957, my father and his new partner, Shama, opened a clothing store they named *el Porvenir*, the Future. Located in the Lawton neighborhood (named for Batista's secretary), they sold clothing for men, women, and children. The store was located about three miles from the city center and boasted the estate of Fernando Batista. The business was extremely successful since their closest competition was over five miles away.

Despite the store's great success, customers were often frustrated because Shama had trouble communicating with them. Shama's Spanish was a disaster, and he often interjected his Spanish sentences with Polish, Russian, and Yiddish. Shifra and my parents often took over for Shama when the customers needed rescue. After speaking to Shama, customers looked at my mother with an expression that equaled, "What did he say?" and we had a great laugh. I suspect that jealousy was an issue for Shama because customers often asked for my father, who spoke better Spanish, albeit with a Russian accent.

In those days, drinking while working was the norm. My father might have an occasional beer, but Shama enjoyed drinking on a regular basis, understandable considering his tormented past. He would steal away for a shot of Cuban rum at a bar next door. There was another local bar near the store, but Shama didn't dare go there. Known as El Cangrejito, the Little Crab, this bar was a hangout for prostitutes.

According to a historical record entitled "Zonas de tolerancia,"[4] prostitution was illegal in Cuba but was overlooked by the bribed police-

4 Hamilton, Carrie. Sexual Revolutions in Cuba: Passion, Politics, and Memory. UNC Press Books, Mar 12, 2012

men. Medical doctors even made regular house calls giving checkups to ensure that these women stayed healthy. They operated out of homes that were converted to houses of ill repute, known by everyone as "Tolerance Zones." They were located in such places as El Barrio de Pajarito and Barrios de Hornos. In fact, there were several such operations only a few blocks from our apartment in Havana on La Calle Anima. These brothels were intermingled with family homes. To prevent intrusion by unwanted gentlemen visitors, placards were put in the windows of these family homes that read, *No molestar. Esta es una casa decente* (Do not bother. This is a decent house).

The ladies of the night frequented our store on Saturdays, coming in groups of six or more. My mother had a knack for dealing with these women. She knew their occupation, and eccentric taste in clothing. Yet, despite her own strict moral compass, she showed them the utmost respect. In turn, these women grew to love my mother's warmth and sympathy. They had expensive tastes and never haggled over the prices. My mother always commented that their most popular purchase was red underpants with lace.

Me, a Thief?

One Saturday night in 1957, I was helping out in my father's store. We always closed between seven and eight in the evening. As was customary, my father and Shama checked the cash register to make sure the balance was correct. It came up short and they soon discovered that money was missing from the cash register. Shama immediately blamed me for stealing the money. That didn't sit well with my father. I remember the scene like a movie. My father yelled at Shama in Yiddish, "*Zenen ir fakh meyn zun a ganof?* Are you calling my son a thief?" In a fit of rage, my dad proceeded to grab Shama by the neck. I thought he was going to kill him, but my father finally relented.

That evening after searching again, the money turned up. It was misplaced under the wooden register tray. Eventually, all was forgiven and forgotten between the two men, but not for me. It was a snapshot in time

I can never put behind me. I knew that my father would always have my back.

There was only one other incident where I can remember my father losing his temper to the point of violence. It was around two o'clock, and the store was usually busy with housewives and their older daughters browsing the dresses and other articles and goods. My father, ever the watchful guard, spotted a man trying to steal merchandise. Despite his short stature of five foot four and weight of 160 pounds, my father had incredible physical strength and was afraid of no one (except my mother). He confronted the shoplifter, and found the stolen goods, stuffed inside the man's own clothing. An argument quickly ensued, and as the conflict escalated, it moved outside where my father punched this man square in the face. I don't remember seeing the damage, but I do recall watching the foiled thief run away, never to be seen again.

Seventeen

Political Unrest

Cuba followed the European educational system, combining high school and college. Known as the school of baccalaureate, we began learning our advanced degrees early. Like my parents, I too had the aptitude for easily memorizing facts and understanding information. I graduated with straight As, ready to attend medical school. Unfortunately, my graduation year collided with the last year of Batista's presidency. In order to understand why the Cuban political landscape was so frail in 1957, we need to rewind to 1952, the year when Cuban politics became littered with turmoil, unrest, imprisonment, torture, and murder...

1952: Batista's Coup d'Etat

Cuba was a young republic that gained independence from Spain on May 20, 1902, after the Spanish-American War. Cuba had since known only a few true democratic governments. The physician Dr. Ramón Grau San-Martine governed one such democracy. He served as Cuba's president in 1933–1934 and 1944–1948. His successor was president Carlos Prío Socarrás.

On March 10, 1952, Fulgensio Batista, a general in the Cuban army took over the Socarrás government in a military-forced coup d'etat.

That year marked the beginning of Cuba's long and lonely darkness that pervades to this day. It started with Batista's dictatorship, which widened the gap between the wealthy and poor. His corruption was boundless. He befriended American mobsters like Meyer Lansky and Lucky

Luciano in an effort to profit from casino earnings and narcotics traf-
ficking. His personal Swiss bank account and those of his cronies was
purported to be in the millions. It was a toxic mix of the Wild West and
good old-fashioned mafia, Latin style. Batista squashed any perceived
opposition, real or imagined, and he did it with extreme brutality. When
asked to analyze the danger of the political situation in Cuba, US histo-
rian and presidential advisor Arthur M. Schlesinger Jr. said, "The corruption of the Government, the brutality of the police, the government's
indifference to the needs of the people for education, medical care,
housing, for social justice and economic justice…is an open invitation
to revolution."[5]

His analysis was prophetic, and by January 1, 1959, a young lawyer
trained in guerilla warfare, Fidel Castro, overthrew Batista. Initially,
Castro hid his real political agenda, but we all knew the truth, and in a
few years, he started showing his true "red" colors. In the early 1960s he
announced that he was indeed a communist or, as he liked to call himself, a Marxist-Leninist. In view of the unstable political situation caused
by his ideologies, enraged upper- and middle-class Cubans started to
emigrate, primarily to the United States of America.

These Cuban émigrés found the democracy, freedom, and peace
they so ardently desired. Meanwhile, in the name of communism, Castro
began his greedy takeover of the country by confiscating all types of businesses and properties, including his own mother's sugar plantation and
my brother-in-law's print shop. When I think about it, it was truly history repeating itself. The Spanish monarchy did it to the Jews, Muslims,
and heretics in the sixteenth century. The Nazis did it to anyone who
opposed them. And now the Cuban communist government was the sole
owner of the entire country. Anyone who opposed them was imprisoned
or put to death by firing squad.

But it was during the years from 1952–1959 that being a young adult
of university age was extremely dangerous, and my own young adulthood

---

5 The Dynamics of World Power: A Documentary History of the United States Foreign
Policy 1945-1973, by Arthur Meier Schlesinger, 1973, McGraw-Hill, ISBN 0070797293, p. 512

fell right into that gap of time. Student involvement in political change was common in Latin American countries and in Cuba even more so. My family and friends have a difficult time comprehending why and how students were involved in actual governmental change on any level. The American public seems very apolitical from a proactive stance. They may grumble and complain, but they are essentially laissez-faire. But in those times, young people were always at the forefront of Cuban politics, and students at the University of Havana led the charges and demonstrations protesting the Batista dictatorship.

For myself, as a student at the University of Havana, I was only interested in academic pursuits; I couldn't have cared less about politics. Staying out of the fight, I believe my perspective as a frontline observer was unique. Here is what I experienced:

I remember that in the early fifties, students joined different organizations, and all of them were politically oriented. Regardless of affiliation, nearly every student wanted a democratic government, and the Batista dictatorship was far from democratic. The university students were outraged, and joining student political groups became popular. I often witnessed the recruitment whenever I traveled by city bus to the beach or to see my medical doctor at the clinic. The bus route always traveled by the University of Havana, and I saw students handing out flyers on the steps of the school. I never belonged to any student organization, and I was too young to be recruited.

One of the biggest groups at the University of Havana was the strongly communist Federación Estudiantíl Universitaria (FEU), the University Students' Federation. Julio Antonio Mella, who originally created FEU, was a cofounder of the Cuban Communist Party in the 1920s. Like many, I was blissfully unaware of the FEU socialist agenda. I just knew that students my age were being mercilessly gunned down in the streets. Once Batista gained power in 1952, I remember violent clashes in the streets between the Cuban police and university students. It was scary because Batista went on the offensive, pursuing, arresting, torturing, and killing students. Despite being a public college, the Universidad de La Habana was always autonomous, considered off-limits to the government and a safe haven for students involved in political unrest. It was a demilitarized zone of sorts, but Batista violated that unwritten rule, and more than once, his police stormed the university, arresting and killing students. The notorious brown Chevys of the *Servicio Intelligensia Militar* (SIM), the military intelligence police service, patrolled, followed, and plucked any suspicious young people and student members of the FEU off the streets. These kids were summarily tortured and killed. Their bodies were dumped in the streets of Havana as a warning to others. Batista exercised the ruthlessness of a medieval warlord; his American mafia friends and their tactics had nothing on El General.

I even had my own scare with the thugs of the SIM. It was 1957, the year I graduated from high school. I was seventeen. Just after graduation, my father had opened his new retail clothing business with Shama. Prior to their grand opening, they had to prepare the shop and spruce it up. My father asked me to help paint. It was a summer morning, I guess around six o'clock. I walked the two blocks in downtown Havana from our apartment building to the nearest bus stop carrying a can of paint in each hand. I was feeling great.

High school was over, the summer was here, and I could luxuriate for two months until it was time to begin medical school. The streets were empty, and the sun was now above the horizon, bright in my eyes and warm on my skin. But my mood suddenly changed. Through my squinting eyes it suddenly appeared: a brown Chevy with blackened windows, one of the unmistakable cars belonging to the SIM. These were Batista's roving gang of enforcers; thugs who snatched young people off the streets, tortured them, and dumped their mutilated corpses in the gutters.

I was terrified. My heart was pounding. I started to sweat, and my mouth went dry. I pretended not to see them, staring down at the ground instead. Making eye contact with them was tantamount to the Latin version of disrespect, challenging them, daring them, and for this alone I would have been arrested.

The car drove up to the sidewalk and moved very slowly. They were observing me. I continued on my way, trying to act as normal as possible.

I knew of their suspicious nature and their erratic, unpredictable methods of yanking anyone off the street to disappear forever. I could feel these murderers staring at me. It seemed like forever, but eventually the car slowly pulled away from the curb and went on its way. When I got to the store, I told my father what had happened. He was beside himself. He kept repeating the words, "You could have gotten in big trouble."

I answered each time in a whisper with, "I know." We both knew. I was lucky to be alive.

As if tensions weren't already heightened, political conditions became alarmingly dangerous. The political violence arm of the FEU was known as the *Directorio Revolucionario* (DR). It was an underground paramilitary group founded in 1955 by the beloved, tall, heavy-set FEU student leader Jose Antonio Echeverria. We all knew Echeverría by his nickname "Manzanita", (Little-Apple) because his face was always a pinkish red. Manzanita was bolstered to act based on a secret meeting in Mexico with Fidel Castro.

The students of the DR were deep in preparation to overthrow the government, and they devised a two-pronged approach. An assault team would storm the presidential palace and assassinate Batista. Meanwhile another group, headed by Echeverría, would overtake Radio Reloj, the Clock Radio station. They would announce the death of Batista and open elections for a new government. Menelao Mora, a man in his forties, helped the students organize the plot, and he was part of the invading force that would dispatch Batista. We knew him personally because his daughter, Amada Mora, was my classmate.

The plot failed. Batista was moved to a safe room in the upper levels of the palace. The presidential guards killed Mora and the other invaders. Meanwhile the police stormed the radio station and killed every student, including Manzanita, who was slain during a getaway.

When we finished high school, we all decided to suspend graduation ceremonies in respect of Mora's death. Fifty years later, our graduation ceremony was celebrated in Miami at the Instituto Edison. All received a diploma. The principal of our school, Ana Maria Rodriguez Gutierrez, died, so her daughter Anita officiated.

We Cubans are famous for coming up with our own conspiracy theories, and I am no exception. I believe that while the children bang the drums, the grown-ups compose the music. Groups like FEU and the DR were simply pawns in a life-and-death game of political chess. Echeverría foolishly believed that his meeting with Castro in Mexico was a meeting of equals and that he would be the great student hero and redeemer of the Cuban people. But Castro wanted to defeat Batista by himself and be viewed as the true liberator of Cuba. It has even crossed my mind that Castro, through intermediaries, warned Batista of the impending student plot. Strangely enough, Castro publicly condemned the plot.

With mounting terror of future assassination attempts, Batista's paranoia grew. He ordered the university closed, and surrounded himself with brutes and criminals who were ready to give their lives for him. These goons subjugated the population with severity. One such example was Batista's appointment of Colonel Antonio Blanco Rico as chief of police. This guy was a notorious thug who indiscriminately killed anyone suspected of subversive activities, especially young students of university age.

However, a dominated people will eventually lash out and lash out they did. I vividly remember the incident: it was the night of October 26, 1956, and Colonel Antonio Blanco Rico was enjoying an evening in the Montmartre, one of Havana's nightclubs. A four-man DR hit squad was in the club led by medical student Rolando Cubela. They were actually hunting for a member of Batista's governmental cabinet, Minister of the Interior, Santiago Rey Pernas. They waited by the elevator, and when it opened, Colonel Blanco Rico walked out. It wasn't the guy they were looking for, but Blanco Rico would certainly do. The group sprayed automatic fire, assassinating him in the lobby. Needless to say, Batista's henchmen and those times bring back horrible memories.

Eighteen

C astro's fight picked up where the students left off. After defeating the Cuban army in the remote mountains and jungles, he moved his guerilla forces to the cities. Batista continued jailing and killing young people because we were all suspected of being in favor of Castro. In 1957, at the peak of political unrest in Cuba, my parents were afraid for my life. As my mother put it, "You'll end up dead in the gutter." They sent me to the United States on a three-month tourist visa, and I stayed in Forest Hills, Queens, New York with my father's brother, my uncle Leo, and his wife, aunt Francis.

Upon my arrival in New York, I quickly realized how sorely I was lacking in the ability to speak conversational English. In Cuba, English was taught as a foreign language beginning in the 4th grade. It was mainly English grammar, not conversational English. In Cuba, my favorite English teacher was the movie theaters of Havana; I watched American movies spoken in English with Spanish subtitles. But I was still very limited in my English speaking abilities. Now that I was in the United States, I had no choice but to speak the native language. In fact, Leo and Francis would not speak to me in Spanish. They insisted I speak English.

To hone my English skills, I would watch a lot of television. My absolute favorites were game shows like the "$64,000 Question" and "What's My Line". I loved "Dragnet," "Candid Camera," and "The Ed Sullivan Show". That summer, Ed Sullivan hosted Louis Armstrong, The Everly Brothers and Johnny Mathis. His guests were the best of the best and once you got on that show, you had it made. On Saturday mornings, my English teachers included the likes of Bugs Bunny, Huckleberry Hound, and Quick Draw McGraw. Movies like "The Ten Commandments" and "The Bridge on the River Kwai" forced me to carefully listen. It was a trial-by-fire total linguistic immersion, and once I learned the basics, English came easy.

Leo and Francis owned a bungalow in the Catskills that they often rented. When available, we would stay there on the weekends but it was boring. To avoid staying there for the week, I returned with Leo to Queens and took business classes in Jamaica, Long Island. Friday evening he and I would return to the bungalow. Spending time with Leo was very different from spending time with my father. Leo had a cut and dry personality. He would chat, make small talk and other pleasantries whereas my father was a real joker with a highly charismatic personality.

That was a memorable summer, but once my visa expired, I returned to Cuba. My parents needed a new plan, one that would get me out of Cuba permanently.

Nineteen

Charles Gerber, the Angel of New York

Not long after, Charles Gerber, a wealthy garment merchant and his wife, Dorothy, came to our island on a cruise. He was searching for people from his shtetl in Poland and knew my mother was in Cuba. It was forty years since they had seen each other. He called our home, and my mother was thrilled to hear from him. She invited them over for dinner that evening. After the meal, we all retired to the living room. My mother served tea and cookies. The conversation was held in Yiddish, and began like all others for WWII survivors from Eastern Europe: Who survived the concentration camps? Who escaped just in time? Which families and friends survived or perished at the hands of the Nazis and anti-Semitic Poles? Who was alive, and who was dead?

At some point the discussion abruptly changed, and we were discussing the political situation in Cuba. While holding a sugar cube between her teeth, my mother took several sips of tea. With the sugar dissolved, she put the teacup down, took a deep breath and told Charles that she was afraid for my life. Batista was ruthlessly arresting and executing young people right off the streets.

On the flip side, Castro was making a play for power, and like most of the Jews who fled the Bolsheviks, my parents were afraid that Castro would install a communist regime. Caught between a homicidal dictator and a Communist insurgent, she told him emphatically that she would love for me to move to the United States. Permanently. To do that, I'd need a resident visa, commonly known as a green card.

Charles Gerber knew of the grave dangers of political unrest. Using my mother's Yiddish nickname from their childhood, he said, "Sorche, say no more. When I get back to New York, I will start pulling a few strings and send an affidavit on behalf of your son to the American Embassy in Havana. In the meantime, make sure that Pepe fills out a residency visa. I will coordinate the rest." At the end of their visit, this wonderful couple boarded their cruise ship and returned to the United States. It took three of the longest months I could remember, but, sure enough, he was a man of his word. I received my permanent-resident visa and green card. It was the "Willy Wonka Golden Ticket" that allowed me to freely travel between Cuba and the United States.

New Hampshire

Between 1958 and 1959, the University of Havana was still closed, so I decided to come to the United States with the idea of trying to enter medical school. As it turned out, medical schools were very expensive, and I had no money. I located Mike, a friend from Cuba who was living in Boston with family friends. I explained my situation and that I wanted to begin my higher education. Mike was in the same predicament, so we met with a friend of his, the dean of Chelsea high school, Mr. Henry.

Mr. Henry had connections with some of the New England colleges. As a state school in New England, The University of New Hampshire had to accept a certain number of foreign students, and they hadn't yet met their quota. Mr. Henry said we were a shoe-in's and asked what would be my second choice to medicine. This university had an excellent engineering department, and Mike was really gung ho about engineering. So the decision was made for me: engineering would be my runner-up.

We went to the dean of admissions, and he said that we would fit nicely into their program. So I began my freshman year in the engineering department at the University of New Hampshire. Mike and I were dorm roommates, and it was fun sharing a room with someone I trusted who shared my native language and background.

In December, nearing the end of the first semester, I realized that engineering was not for me, and I simply didn't have the desire to continue the program. Reluctantly, I decided to finish the year and reevaluate my options. There were only two available to me: If the University of Havana by some miracle opened, I would attend medical school there. If not, I would reluctantly stay at UNH.

For me, medicine was not just an interest but also a calling, and I'm sure it developed at a very young age. When I was ten months old, I had metabolic acidosis, essentially a death sentence in those times. The chief of medicine held a conference with his colleagues, but they simply had no answers. Metabolic acidosis is not a disease but a biochemical abnormality, and probably why it left the doctors scratching their heads. The medical team told my parents to pray a lot because only a miracle could save me. I was given blood transfusions in both arms and to do so, they had to perform a cut-down of my veins. I somehow survived, but the cut-downs left me permanently scarred, a reminder of how close I came to dying at a young age.

Perhaps it left my body immune-deficient because, as a child, I had chicken pox, measles, and whooping cough. This last malady occurred when Anita was preparing for her wedding. I remember eating a meal, and then coughing so violently that I vomited. There were no antibiotics, only powdered sulfa. I was among the first to receive the polio vaccine in Cuba. The smallpox immunity was being administered in a very crude fashion. Two scratches were made on my leg, the dead smallpox bacteria placed in the wounds, and the site covered with plastic. With the frequent medical visits, I became infatuated with medical care and an admirer of Dr. Alvare, who, to me as a small child, appeared as a demigod. He belonged to the Damas de la Covadonga Clinic on the corner of Seventeenth and *J* in the Vedado District.

With the school year over, the summer of '59 called Mike and I down to Havana for our vacation. With Castro now in power, the University of Havana finally opened, and they were admitting all the students who had graduated high school since 1955. Because I graduated in 1957, I was automatically admitted, but I was unsure if I should enroll. I met some of my friends from high school, and several of them planned to go to medical school. They said I should stay and fulfill my dreams of becoming a physician. After giving it some serious thought, I went to my parents and told them that I was staying. They were unhappy because they knew who Castro was, and they were scared for me to stay in Cuba. I didn't care, and I made my decision to stay. Mike went back to UNH, and I enrolled in medical school at the University of Havana.

Twenty

Should I Stay or Should I Go?

My father told me the only thing you should ever say publically is that Batista was an SOB and that Fidel was our savior. My father began, "If you speak against Fidel, they will put you in front of the firing squad and kill you."

I answered, "Dad, you are seeing ghosts everywhere."

He continued. "I went through this in Russia when Lenin took over. I know who these people are and what they stand for. Castro is a rotten person, and soon you will see who he really is."

Eventually, I saw that my father was totally right, and I was totally wrong. But since all teenagers think they know it all, I thought, *Why do I need this green card if Fidel will fix Cuba?* Without consulting my parents, I went to the American embassy and requested an interview with a consul.

I sat in a small chair outside a thick wooden door. I heard shuffling, and the knob turned. The door opened, and a tall, chubby man in his late forties came out. He was dressed in a polyester suit and tie and had a nice disposition. He ushered me into his office and we sat down in casual, lounge-type chairs. I felt as if I was in this man's home. "Sir," I began. "I want to turn in my visa and green card." I continued explaining that I was planning to stay in Cuba for medical school, and there was no reason for me to have these cards.

He heard my story and looked at me in disbelief. "Where do you keep that green card?" he asked.

"In my wallet," I replied.

His voice became low, almost a deadly whisper, "Is it that heavy that you want to get rid of it?"

I said sheepishly, "No," and hung my head, staring at the plush green carpet.

He continued, "I'm going to forget that you came here, and ignore this conversation."

I remained silent, feeling stupid. He escorted me out, shook my hand, and wished me the best of luck. With a wink, he turned around and was gone. Later on I realized that he had saved my life, because I wouldn't have been able to come to the United States, and if my parents had found out, my mother would have done worse things to me than Castro could ever do. She would have chopped me to pieces.

Medical School

It was September 1959, and I started my first year of medical school at the University of Havana. Because of the long shut down, there were four years of high-school graduating classes waiting to begin medical school. That year, the freshman class size was massive.

Universidad de La Habana

To excel, we formed study groups. There were four guys and one girl in my group, and we would often meet at her house after school hours. Her father was a well renowned pathologist at one of the University hospitals in Havana. His name was Ramon "Mongo" Vidal, and his wife Llillina ("Gigina"). He was a great guy, and we all had a crush on his beautiful wife. I remember they had a Doberman pinscher. Her mother always served us snacks with Cuban coffee at around ten at night. Academically, our group became one of the top performers in anatomy.

My study group would often end late into the evening and it was common for me to come home around one in the morning. Before going home, I walked to the corner across the street from my apartment building. There, a vendor with a pushcart sold *fritas,* a Cuban version of the hamburger. The vendor would fry mystery meat and stuff it inside a roll with thin shoestring fries, tomatoes and some other spices. My mother was sure that the combination of eating this concoction before bed would kill me or at the very least give me a good case of dysentery. But I loved those fritas and they never made me sick.

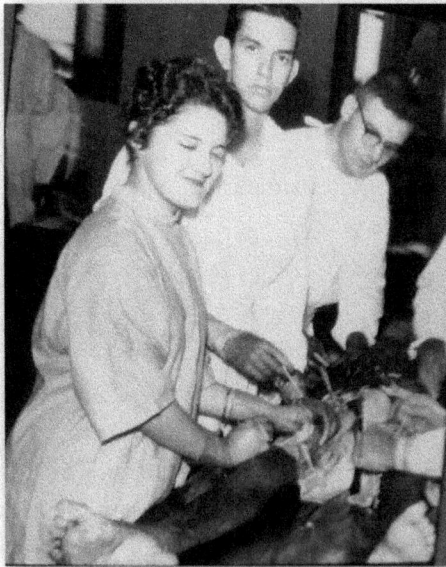

My study group doing human dissection in
anatomy lab, University of Havana, 1959.
L to R: Tulia (Vidal) Benazer, Raul Villasuso, Me.

When I was in my first year of medical school in Havana, we had a subject that was compulsory: medical psychology. The course required that we take a class trip deep inside the Cuban countryside and interview the peasants. Historically, the peasant class received little if any medical care. We were told to gauge their psychological approach to the socio-political and medical situation in the countryside. What this had to do with psychiatry was anyone's guess. It was more likely a political outreach attempt by Fidel's good people.

Cuban peasants were often left to fend for themselves. They were completely self-reliant, growing their own produce and living in their one-room *bohios*, homes with a round structure (like those built in many primitive societies around the world). The *bohios* were constructed of straw walls, palm leaf roofs and packed dirt floors. There was no electricity or running water. At night, lanterns were used, kind of like the Amish, Caribbean style. They slept on hammocks strung across the wall. Washing was done in local streams. The often-large broods helped with chores; girls did housework and boys tended the field. The death rate was high, and children often died from tropical diseases or typical childhood illnesses like the measles.

Organized in a group of nine, we traveled in military trucks painted olive-green, the signature color of Castro's army. Our group traveled to the end of the most Western part of Cuba, Pinar Del Rio province, near the Yucatan Peninsula. More specifically, we were in an area known as Peninsula De Guanahacabibes, named centuries ago by the indigenous Guanahatabeyes people. We were housed in primitive army barracks and slept in wooden bunk beds with thin mattresses. On that first night, the mosquitoes feasted, and we barely slept. Over the next two days, bleary-eyed and sore, we interviewed a local family. It was common practice to speak with the most important member of the family, and in Cuba, that was the husband. Our main question was, "Are you happy with the new regime, specifically the improvements in medical care?" The husband seemed optimistic, expecting big changes. In reality, change never came.

The poorer classes generally relied on home remedies using plants and roots. This was common practice in Cuba, and reminded me of the folk medical treatment I received as a child. I was five, and it was the summer of 1944. I contracted chicken pox, and initially I improved, but a few days later, I developed a fever. My mother called Dr. Alvare, who made a house call. He looked in my mouth, turned to my mother, and said, "Pepe has Koplik's spots, and it is the surest sign that he has measles."

Today we have immunization, but then, it was "wait and see, and hopefully get better." I was kept home from school under quarantine.

Luisa was concerned because the only area the measles showed was in my mouth. Usually, a rash appeared on the body. In her village, it was important that the rash should come out, and if not, it would stay inside the body and wreak havoc. So she went to the market where roots were sold, and she bought *borraja*, also known as starflower. She boiled the roots and ordered me to drink the tincture. Years later, I investigated this traditional practice and discovered something remarkable. Modern western medicine has found it helpful in combating measles, mumps, chicken pox, colds, and flus. *Borraja*, or *Borago officinalis*, has been used to treat gastrointestinal conditions such as colic, cramps, and diarrhea. It is also used to treat respiratory and cardiovascular disorders, such as asthma, bronchitis, hypertension, and blood dyscrasia. For my situation, it was used to reduce my fever and induce sweating, but all I remember is that it tasted bitter and made me want to throw up. Fortunately, I held it down, and sure enough, a few hours later, the rash came out. Folklore demanded that I was to be completely out of the sun or it could affect the eyes and cause blindness. So Luisa covered the windows with heavy sheets, and I stayed in the pitch-black, suffering from the stuffy heat of the tropics. Luisa catered to me, cooked chicken soup, and tried to keep me as comfortable as possible. Ralph brought me comic books, and a week later, I was back to normal.

Twenty-One

Time to Go

From 1959 to 1960, the politics of Cuba were growing more than uneasy. With Castro now in power, the situation was becoming downright dangerous. I had decided that enough was enough and that I had to leave Cuba as soon as possible. In reality, my sympathies were not with the Castro brothers. If this were known, it would imply that I was a counterrevolutionary, a file would be opened, and I could be thrown in jail.

In the spring of 1960, my first year as a medical student came to a close. As was the norm, I walked to the student mail center to check for any notes from friends or the medical journals actually addressed to me. Instead, there was an official-looking sealed envelope with the school's logo. It was addressed to me and was from the office of the registrar. I held the envelope in my hand and walked outside to the steps of the school entrance, hoping a fresh Caribbean breeze would come by and calm me down. I carefully opened the envelope and unfolded the letter. The message was clear and succinct. "The dean of admission has asked for your immediate presence in his office to discuss a certain matter." A certain matter? I gulped hard. That never sounded good, especially with the swirling of dissent among pro-Castro students at the university. And since I didn't believe there were mind readers, no one could have known of my plans. Still, I was edgy.

Nervously I knocked on his door. He asked me to sit down at a chair across from his impressive Spanish style mahogany desk. He sat in his large well-worn leather chair and held a folder with my transcript in his hands. He opened the folder and was probably pretending to review it because I'm sure he had already looked at it. He leaned forward, folded his hands on the desk and addressed me informally. "Pepe, how would you like to attend school next year at no cost to you?" I was flabbergasted. For a brief moment, I was sure he knew of my plans to flee the island. Otherwise, why would he make me the classic *Godfather* offer "I couldn't refuse"?

"We want to give you a full scholarship for next year because of your outstanding grades."

For a moment, I became woozy. This was too much to think about, but I'm sure he thought I would jump at the offer. "Thank you, Doctor. This is a lot to think about," I said. "It's such a generous offer. I must present this to my parents before I can accept this gift." *Quick thinking, Jose,* I mused.

He sat back and smiled. "Of course. Of course. That is no problem. The offer won't run away. Just speak to your parents. I'm sure they will be thrilled with the news."

I replied, "Oh yes. I'm sure they will be thrilled," keeping the sarcasm out of my voice.

When I arrived home that day, I sat my parents down, showed them the letter, and told them of the offer. They were obviously extremely proud and yet saddened at the same time. My sentiments were reflected, and we all sat quietly for what seemed an eternity. Later that week, I returned to his office to decline the offer so it would be available to another student. It was the right thing to do. I informed him that I was no longer interested in continuing my studies. He looked at me as though I were insane, but he asked no questions. Silence. I knew that my rejection might reveal my real intentions, but he said nothing. I thanked him again, and said my good-byes.

I sighed and walked down those grand whitewashed steps of the University of Havana School Of Medicine, never to return again.

Emigration from Cuba

At this point, the entire family knew that we had to leave Cuba for good, but how? The Castro government was becoming more aware of those fleeing, and a large family would have raised alarms. We would have to leave under the guise of vacation travel, with only a few of us at a time, purchasing round-trip tickets to the United States, never intending to return to Havana.

At the end of 1959, the first to leave was Anita, together with her husband Raphael (we called him Ralph in the United States) and their two boys, Willy and Milton.

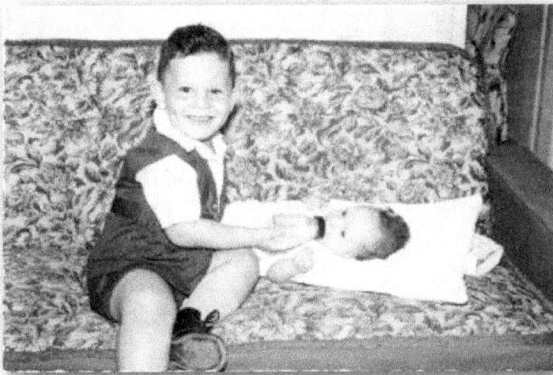

My nephews Willy and Milton Bondar

My nephew Milton's second birthday party

They landed in Washington DC, and since Ralph knew the printing business, he got a job at the Washington Post. Because he was a new employee, he was assigned the graveyard shift.

My nephews standing outside a subway
platform in Brooklyn, New York, 1960

Anita was upset that they had to abandon the printing shop in Cuba. After all, they had outfitted the place with over $50,000 in machinery alone. She convinced Ralph she was going to sell the shop and the machines. Ralph was upset and said to let Castro have it. But my sister was strong-willed, and she and her boys returned to Havana in a desperate attempt to sell her husband's printing shop. After they arrived, they stayed with us in our apartment. She brought her sons, thinking that her stay in Cuba would be a short one and she would be able to sell the printing shop rather quickly. My mother was absolutely incensed at her for returning to Cuba. Once the printing-shop workers were made aware of her return, they went to the Ministry of Labor and accused her of being a counterrevolutionary. That accusation alone carried a sentence of incarceration followed by firing squad.

Unaware of the accusations, Anita decided to take matters into her own hands. At the Ministry of Labor, she met Raphaelito, a high-school classmate who was now an attorney and very anti-Castro. She made him aware of her anger at the Castro government and he decided to help her as much as he could. Not willing to wait for the slow gears of justice, Anita decided to act. The next day she rented a truck and at three in the morning, drove off with all of the printing equipment. She unloaded it in a storage facility and returned to our home.

The next day, police cars surrounded our apartment building and sharp shooters took their positions on the roof of the apartment across the street. Castro wasn't playing around. The message was clear: those who opposed him would be dealt with and treated with a heavy hand. The police immediately arrested Anita and took her away in handcuffs. We were all in shock, and it didn't take us long to realize that we had better start moving quickly if there was any hope of finding my sister alive.

We went to see Raphaelito, the family friend and lawyer. He picked us up in his car, and we drove from one police station to the next. No Anita. We had been at it all day, and now the sun was setting. It was seven o' clock and we were about to give up when we decided to check one last station. The officer in charge said that yes, there was an Anita Bondar in their jail. We all breathed a sigh of relief, but we knew that the really hard part was about to begin. Raphaelito addressed the officer and identified himself as Anita's lawyer. He asked if she had been charged with any wrongdoing. The answer was no, so our intrepid attorney demanded that she be released into his custody. Amazingly, the officer relented, and she was freed. Raphaelito told her in no uncertain terms that she must leave the country at once.

The next morning, Anita called several airlines and found three seats available on a 9:00 a.m. Pan Am flight to Miami, scheduled to fly out in three days. She purchased round-trip tickets so as not to arouse suspicion. Those next three days were tension-filled, and we were convinced she would be arrested again once someone found out she was released. On the day of her departure, we all awoke at 4:00 a.m. Everyone quietly dressed. We sat in our living room, her luggage by the door, silence all around. We arranged for a taxi to pick us up at 6:00 a.m., while it was still dark outside. We rode to the airport in complete silence. Even my rambunctious young nephews were aware of the peril and stayed quiet. We all prayed that no one we knew would see us at the airport.

Jose Marti Airport circa 1955

On arrival to Havana's Jose Marti Airport, Anita and her boys were separated from us and placed in what was commonly known as the "fish tank," a room with glass windows that only passengers can enter. Finally her flight was called, and we waved good-bye. We went upstairs to the outdoor terrace deck, facing the airfield. We could see the passengers as they exited the terminal, walked out on the tarmac, and climbed the stairway into their airplane.

Once all the passengers were aboard, the door was closed, and the four engine propellers of the Pan Am DC-7 began to turn. We waited with anticipation and anxiety for the plane to taxi down the sole runway, but the stairway was not moved and the roaring plane remained still. Suddenly we noticed an easily identifiable "secret" police car approach the aircraft, stopping right by the stairway. The door to the plane was opened, and a flight attendant in a bright-blue uniform appeared. The police attempted to board the airplane. We couldn't hear what transpired, but we were alarmed. With a deep sinking feeling, we thought they were going to haul Anita out of the plane. A few moments later, a different woman appeared. She exited the door at the top of the stairway, and upon reaching the tarmac, was escorted by these policemen to their car and whisked away.

Finally the door to the plane closed, the stairway was moved, and the DC-7 took a position on the runway and was, at last, airborne. My parents and I faced each other, and we broke out in tears. The date was June 1960. In less than half an hour, my sister and nephews were flying over the Straits of Florida. Soon Key West would become visible, and after another twenty minutes, they landed at Miami International Airport. At long last they were finally free and safe.

Once she landed safely in Miami, Anita told us what happened. The secret police had orders to take this woman into custody. However, that airliner, bound for Miami was considered US territory. In order to board the aircraft, these policemen would have to seek permission from the US consulate. To circumvent this, one of the officers apparently leaned over to the flight attendant and whispered in her ear the name of the passenger who was forbidden to leave Cuban territory. The flight attendant asked the woman to step off the aircraft. Sadly, this happened all too often.

Twenty-Two

Fleeing Cuba

After Anita left, I was mentally tortured about what the future had in store for me in Cuba. My parents and I were sure it wouldn't take the government long to associate me with my defector sister, and now my life was in danger. So in September 1960, I started to arrange my own departure from Cuba. I booked a flight on Cubana de Aviación airlines for October 28, 1960. Entering the United States would not be problematic because I already had a permanent-resident visa (green card). I couldn't tell anyone in my study group that I was leaving. Word would get around, and "they" would try to stop me from leaving the country. My departure was shrouded in total secrecy, as everything was at that time in Cuba. My classmates were not to be told of my plans under any circumstances.

There is no question that Cuba was a fantastic country and that Havana was a fabulous city. Under normal circumstances I would have never left. I would have made my life in that tropical paradise. I left Cuba because I saw the writing on the wall. It was clear who Castro actually was and what he was attempting to do. Fidel Castro was to become *El Dictator Maximo*, lord and master of the entire country of Cuba. Like Anita had done, I too departed under the cover of early-morning darkness, boarding a taxi with my parents. The scene was déjà-vu. I waited in the fish tank with the other passengers, turned, and waved good-bye to my parents. I acted as normally as I could, boarded the Super-G Constellation Cubana de Aviación airplane, and departed from Havana without any problems.

As the plane started to climb, I looked out the window at Havana for one last time. Havana was my city, the city where I had spent the

The Cubana de Aviación Lockheed Super Constellation airplane

best years of my life, and I knew I would never see it again as long as the Castros remained in power. While the plane was still flying over Cuban airspace, the entire cabin remained in eerie, complete silence. Apparently, I wasn't the only one saying good-bye forever.

Close to five hours later, we landed in New York's Idlewild Airport (made famous by the great Lufthansa heist in the movie *Goodfellas*), now known as J. F. K. International. Some passengers began singing the Cuban national anthem, *"El Himno de Bayamo," "La Bayamesa,"* the Bayamo Anthem. Others wept, and whether they were tears of joy or tears of sadness, it did not matter. All of our lives were now permanently altered. My sister, Anita, and Ralph were waiting for me at the gate. The next project was to get our parents out of Cuba.

When anyone decided to leave the country, they could not say good-bye to their friends and classmates for fear of being detained. I had already been gone for several weeks, and the members of my study group from medical school were wondering what happened to me. One day, they came to our apartment and yelled down from the street for Pepe. My mother heard the shouting for her son. She hesitated, then steeled herself and walked out to the terrace. She looked down and bravely smiled. "Good morning. How is everyone?" she asked.

The classmates were respectful and offered polite exchanges. One of them asked, *"Dónde está Pepe?"*

My mother replied, *"Pepe no está aquí* (Pepe isn't here)."

"Where is he?" they asked.

My mother just smiled again, and remained silent. She was caught off-guard and didn't know how to reply. If she told the truth, she would be accused of being a counterrevolutionary. They immediately realized that her silence could only mean I had flown the coop. My name was placed on a bulletin board at the medical school as a traitor to *la patria*, the fatherland. Amazingly the government never retaliated against my parents.

Mr. Shapiro: Danger All Around

In August 1960, only a few months before my departure, some alarming news flashed through the Jewish community. An important American citizen, businessman, leader of the United Hebrew Congregation, and long-time Havana resident was the target of violence. Charles Shapiro, my mother's first employer, owner of the textile factory in Guanabacoa and *Los Precios Fijos*, one of Havana's largest department stores, fell victim to the political crisis. Five armed Cubans broke into the Shapiro home. Ten family members, including Charles; his wife, Wilma; and several servants, were beaten and tied up. The robbers looted the house, taking all of the money and jewelry they could find. Coincidentally, their department store was set ablaze at the same time they were being robbed. With evidence pointing to the attacks being anti-Semitic in nature, the Jews were naturally nervous about staying in the country.

Twenty-Three

Life in New York

I stayed with Anita and Ralph in their apartment in the west Bronx. I found employment at the Sloan Kettering Memorial Cancer Research Hospital in the biology lab. Once again, I was in the medical field and found it fascinating. I worked there for a few months but needed more money, so I applied for a job at Beekman Hospital, located in the financial district of lower Manhattan. As nice as it was working at a hospital, the income was paltry. I required a substantial increase to pay for my studies in medicine, and a hospital income wasn't enough. So I found a new job at a coffee company in Jamaica, New York that paid the money I needed for future tuition.

I worked in the quality-control laboratory during the night shift from eleven to seven. The place never shut down. One of my duties was to taste the coffees being brewed. It was a "sip and spit" deal, and soon my taste buds became refined enough to tell if the public would like the coffee or not. The responsibility was huge, because if I was wrong, the company could lose a fortune in revenue. After my night shift, I went home, slept for a few hours, and then worked on my applications to various medical schools. One of the schools that interested me was the University of Florida College of Medicine at Gainesville. It was founded in 1956 by the dean, Dr. George T. Harrell Jr., a progressive thinker in medical education. I found the dean's new concept of training doctors to be intriguing. His goal was for doctors to understand and care for the whole patient, and he advocated the concept of training students in small groups.

When Gainesville notified me of my acceptance I was thrilled. In addition, they accepted my credits from my first year in Havana. I only had to take a physiology course, and it could be at the medical school of my choice. That summer, I enrolled in a physiology course at Columbia University. It was expensive, but for the opportunity to attend a reasonably priced, progressive US medical school, I was willing to pay it. Soon after completing the course at Columbia, I received another notification from admissions that tuition at Gainesville had increased. To me, it had skyrocketed, and I was forced to look elsewhere.

Another school that accepted me was the *Universidad Nacional Autónoma de México* (UNAM), the National Autonomous University of Mexico. Located in Mexico City, this public-research university was the largest in Latin America and the oldest on the continent. They had only two stipulations. The first required that I start school from the first year, which I was willing to do. The second was a bit trickier and revolved around my getting a Mexican visa. The Mexican government was friendly with Castro, and when they saw I was a political refugee from Cuba, they said I would need to deposit $10,000 in a Mexican bank every year for four years for the rights to that visa. Their reasoning was that the money would be used to prevent me from becoming a public charge to their government. Taking into account annual US inflation at 3.9 percent, in today's money, it would be equivalent to nearly $80,000 per year for a grand total of $320,000. For a kid without a dime to his name, this was pure nonsense.

I went to the Mexican Consulate in New York to complain. They said that since I had been accepted to this reputable medical school, I had better deposit the $10,000 in order to obtain a Mexican visa. Adios, Mexico!

But I was not down for the count just yet, and even if the Americas wouldn't cooperate, I still had several options open in Europe. As chance would have it, I was in Manhattan one afternoon walking down Broadway when I ran into a former medical school classmate from Havana. He said he was continuing medical school in France at the University of Montpelier. He had studied at the Alliance Français in Cuba and was brushing up at a local language-learning center. He was well connected with a young lady who represented the student union in Paris at la Sorbonne. He wrote her name and phone number on some scrap paper and suggested I call her if I was ever in Paris. I thanked him, and we parted ways.

I folded that paper away in my wallet and thought nothing more of it. I decided to continue submitting applications to various schools overseas. I sent a letter to the Ministry of Education in Spain with my transcripts, and they said my records from Cuba were outstanding, and they'd credit me for my first year of medical school. So off to Spain I went.

Twenty-Four

Fleeing Cuba — My Parents

While I was taste-testing coffee during the wee hours, my parents were working on their escape from Cuba. One day, there was a knock on the door to my parents' apartment. The man spoke to my father in Russian. He was a representative from the Russian newspaper Pravda.

Besides being a smart businessman, my father was a keen observer of affairs of state. He was able to gauge the political winds and somehow early on, he intuitively knew that one day he would have to leave the country, perhaps based on his own history with the Russians. Luckily he knew how to gain favor among the newly empowered communists, especially those in the *Comités de Defensa de la Revolución* (CDR), the Committees for the Defense of the Revolution. This was an organization created by Fidel Castro himself, an idea he stole directly from Adolf Hitler's 1935 "Committees of Territorial Vigilance". In essence, these were neighborhood-watch programs that were headed by the lowest of the low. It was an opportunity for the down-and-outs, the dregs of society, to have a voice and flex their power. These were the people on whom the revolution was founded; people who operated at the margins of society; people who, prior to Castro, had contributed nothing to humanity. They were the eyes and ears of the revolution at the grass-roots level, reporting any counterrevolutionary activity to the government.

But my father knew how to deal with these people. Since his store was in a middle-class neighborhood, it grew as a hotbed of CDR activity. My father was able to garner favor with these dangerous simpletons by giving away pairs of pants, shirts, and even underwear. It was primarily because of my father's genius in dealing with them that they approved him to leave the country whenever he decided. In most cases, after someone signed a petition to leave the country, it often took years to receive consent. My father received his permit in just three months.

It was now my parents' turn to quickly get ready to flee. They had saved cash but couldn't take it out of the country. My mother decided to convert the cash into goods. She had the finest custom clothes made by their seamstress, and went to the best shoe stores in Havana that still had fancy shoes from the pre-Castro days. But while waiting the three months for their travel approval, changes were happening fast in the country. Two months before her departure, the government changed the law that anyone leaving the country could only take three changes of clothing. My mother was crestfallen. She gave away all the clothes and shoes to friends who were staying behind. Almost overnight, the government devalued the Cuban peso to one tenth of its worth, when Che Guevara was president of the Cuban National Bank. My father's entire savings of $100,000 was now a mere $10,000. All those years of hard work and saving money to be worth a tenth!

People don't really understand what went on there, but what Castro did in those days was unbelievable. My father saved as much of the old currency as he could and buried it in the ground, hoping to reclaim it once it regained its value.

A lot of people did that in those days. Many hid their valuables inside the walls of their homes. When money continued to drop to a thirteenth of its original value, Many Jews who were escaping exchanged their Cuban currency for American dollars on the black market and gave it to people who had access to American banks. And my father's buried stash? To this day, no one knows where it is.

Twenty-Five

1962: Spain

While my parents were salvaging what they could and orchestrating their departure from Cuba, I was boarding a flight to Spain on Air France with a one-day layover in Paris. It was a Sunday in the summer of 1962 when I arrived at the Charles de Gaulle Airport. The city was beautiful in June. The weather was warm and dry, very different from the ugly humidity of New York and the ever-changing tropical systems in Cuba. I hailed a cab and went directly to my hotel, located on the left bank of the Seine River. I remembered having the contact information of the young lady who represented the student union in Paris at la Sorbonne. My well-connected friend I had bumped into on a street in New York gave it to me.

I took out my wallet and removed the folded piece of scrap paper that had her name and phone number. I called this lady, (whose name I don't remember) and explained who I was. For good measure, I mentioned my friend's name as a referral. She offered to pick me up at my hotel. We went to the famous La Sorbonne Medical School and met with the dean. I showed him my transcripts, and he accepted me with the provision that I start from the first year. I was actually willing to do that for an opportunity to attend this prestigious institution. However, there was still that sticking point of tuition money and living expenses.

My next and immediate project was to investigate if the United Nations could help me as a political refugee. We spoke to the international refugee committee who informed me that unfortunately, Cubans who were escaping the Castro government were not yet classified as political refugees. They explained that for now, the Castro government had been recognized as legitimate and that it might change in the future. They couldn't channel any funds for my study in France. It was disappointing but actually eased my mind that Spain was the right decision. Adieu France.

The next day, I boarded my flight from Paris to Madrid. After landing in Madrid, I walked through the newly completed airport. It was magnificent. I walked the long corridor, and after going through passport control, I was intercepted by several officials dressed impeccably in Italian-cut suits. They seated me in a small sparse room with a table and chairs. "What was your purpose to this trip?" they asked.

I answered, "It was to complete my medical education."

They politely reminded me that I was here for my education and not to get mixed up in Spanish politics.

"Sir" I said, "I have absolutely no intention of doing that."

We shook hands and they wished me well but I walked a bit shaken to arrivals. The reason I was nervous was because at the time, Spain was under the regime of the fascist dictator, Francisco Franco. This was the same guy who publicly stood up to Hitler's attempt to take over Gibraltar, maintaining complete control of all ships entering the Mediterranean.

In actuality, many believe he had a secret agreement with Hitler. Franco could maintain control of his country without interference from the Nazis. In exchange, the Luftwaffe would land and refuel their warplanes in the Spanish highlands on their way to bomb Great Britain. In addition, if they lost the war, Hitler and his personal guards would be given clandestine asylum and safe passage through Spain on their way to South America.

At arrivals two people greeted me. One was a young fellow my age, the son of our landlord in the building we lived in in Havana. He and his family moved back to Spain after Castro. Also waiting was Manuel Alfonso Ortega, a good friend and classmate of my cousin Ari Pienick. Ari was born in Ecuador, and his sister was a pediatrician there. Ari and Manuel became aeronautical engineers, graduating from Boeing University in Seattle.

When I told Ari that I was going to Spain, he contacted Manuel, who would help me any way he could. I introduced the landlord's son and Manuel at the airport. Manuel had a car and drove me to a boarding house that the landlord's son found for me.

Manuel picked me up later that evening and took me to the Tapas Bars. With every tapas treat, they served a glass of wine or beer. At the end of the evening, he drove me back to the boarding house. I was half drunk, and between the wine, tapas, and jet lag, I was asleep within minutes. The next day I rode the trolley to the ministry of education. I arrived there with my letter of acceptance to medical school at the University of Madrid and all of my transcripts. They said that they could recognize all my subjects except for microbiology, because in Spain they took it together with parasitology. In Cuba, because of the climate and the tropical diseases that plagued the jungles, parasitology was a full-year course by itself.

I had to validate my Cuban records at the ministry of education in order to enroll in medical school. Standing behind me in line were two guys who introduced themselves, Abraham Shmukler, an Ashkenazi Cuban Jew and Marcos Barrocas, a Sephardic Cuban Jew. They were older than me and only needed a few credits to finish medical school. They offered me advice as, overhearing my name, they gathered I was a *landsman,* a fellow Jewish. They said that the Spanish people are nice, warm, and welcoming but there is still an undercurrent of anti-Semitism. They told me not to offer the fact that I was Jewish because I never know what professor might be anti-Semitic and could give me a rough time.

Medical School

The University of Madrid is one of the oldest colleges in the world. It was established on May 20, 1293, and by 1509, it had a world-class medical school. This ancient institution attracted some of the most brilliant minds in medicine. It boasted famous alumni such as Nobel Prize recipients Dr. Santiago Ramon y Cajal in neuroscience and Dr. Severo Ochoa in medicine. That tradition continued when I attended: many of my professors were famous in the world of medicine. They were also real characters. One memorable teacher was the director of biochemistry, Professor Jorge Tamarit-Rodriguez. He was an early pioneer in diabetic research, and like any genius, he had his quirks. Tamarit, as we called him was notorious for failing students. Thankfully I was able to transfer my biochemistry credits from Cuba and avoided taking this course.

But my classmates took his class and they told me that when Tamarit walked into the auditorium-sized class on the first day, the student chatter fell silent. He looked to his right, and then to his left. "I would like you all to memorize the faces of your colleagues to your right and to your left, because I can guarantee that you will not see those faces again. I am notorious for being very demanding in my class, and if you don't answer the way I expect, then you will fail." He was quite the confidence booster, but, in those days, it was accepted.

In order to begin my second year, I had to fulfill certain prerequisites required by all Spanish medical schools. They did not accept my physiology credits from Columbia University, so I enrolled in their physiology class. The professor was Antonio Gallegos. Dr. Gallegos was a disciple of the famous Spanish physiologist Dr. Raphael Laurente de No.

Dr. de No received his medical degree from Madrid at the age of twenty-one and was elected to the National Academy of Sciences in 1950. At the time, his textbook, *A Study of Nerve Physiology*, was the de facto bible for neurophysiologists. Like I said, this place had some heavy hitters. Dr. Gallegos had just returned to Madrid after several years of fieldwork at the Rockefeller Institute for Medical Research in New York City. After taking over the physiology department, his main goal was to apply his groundbreaking research to the curriculum. There were no textbooks. He taught from memory and never quoted references. He didn't need to; they were probably all his.

When the final exam came, there were only ten questions, and they dealt with subjects that he never discussed in class. They were based on material he himself was familiar with from his most recent research. Not yet knowing my grade, I continued taking prerequisites, including pharmacology and pathology, and passed those with ease. When Dr. Gallegos gave out the grades, the number of students who passed was minimal. The great majority failed, including me. I couldn't continue because of that failing grade, and I simply had to find out why.

Not knowing the Madridian white-tower culture, I made the critical mistake of requesting that the great Professor Antonio Gallegos review the exam and show me why I received a failing grade. This was considered a huge no-no! Unbeknown to me, I was now questioning his moral turpitude and casting doubt on his integrity. Even worse, it may have been a blow to his machismo. Naïvely, I went to what was known as a "revision of exam." Dr. Gallegos kept it short and sweet. With a smirk, he showed me what I did incorrectly. He leaned toward me in his cramped office and said, "Let's forget you asked me to go over the final with you. Study harder and come back for another final in September."

I could read between the lines. I walked out of that office knowing that I was screwed and that "another final" was code for another failing grade. With no choice, I decided to leave Madrid and enroll in the medical school in Cadiz.

Unlike the landlocked capital, Cadiz is a beautiful seaside town. It is an ancient place and was the site where the famous explorer Christopher Columbus launched his ships. The University of Cadiz was created in the fifteenth century as a nautical college. In 1748, the most important cultural institution ever was created in Cadiz. This was the Royal College of Surgery of the army. Despite the venerable and hallowed halls, the "god syndrome" was absent, and the staff was more amenable to talk to the students and treat them as human beings.

There, I aced physiology but had to repeat pharmacology and pathology, since they were not transferrable from Madrid due to that failing physiology grade. Now ready for my second year, I took internal medicine and surgery. These were courses that were divided into three levels, and each one had to be passed in succession. The professor of surgery, Felipe de la Cruz-Caro, only gave oral exams. During my first exam, he asked me a question that had never been discussed in class, and I was dumbfounded. He asked me a different question, and it was so esoteric, I had no answer. He dismissed me. I failed. My friends in the school knew his reputation for asking impossible questions, yet he often passed students who had connections to the Catholic Church. Knowing his notorious reputation, I knew that it would be impossible to continue with him. A good friend of mine in the school, a Cuban American named Sebastian Rodriguez had to retest three times before he passed. I knew I didn't stand a chance. I decided to transfer to the medical school in Salamanca.

Salamanca is located in northwestern Spain and has the oldest university in Spain. It was founded in 1134 and boasts the alumnus and author of *Don Quixote,* Miguel de Cervantes. Salamanca's weather was very different than other parts of Spain. Because of its altitude it remained relatively cool and dry throughout the year. In addition, the professors there were easier to talk to than in Madrid and Cadiz, and we could have certain connections with the adjunct professor that would help us in our final exams. Finally, in the summer of 1967, I graduated with a medical degree from the University of Salamanca. I can say that in Spain, encountering a corrupt professor was problematic, but I never encountered an overtly anti-Semitic professor.

Twenty-Six

1963: My Parents Flee Cuba

The year was 1963, and tensions between the Kennedy White House and Red Havana were simmering. The Cuban Missile Crisis, and multiple attempts by the US to overthrow the Castro government and/or assassinate him were bungled. The CIA plotted to poison Castro with tainted milkshakes, bacteria-laden wet suits (Castro loved scuba diving), and exploding cigars filled with enough TNT to take his head off. In all, over 600 attempts were made on Fidel's life, none of them successful. At this point, détente was an impossibility and any discussion between the two states was mediated by Switzerland.

My mother was desperate to escape the madness so Anita applied for mama's US visa. Anita went to the United Hebrew Immigrant Aid Society (HIAS), one of three religious agencies now funded by the US government specifically to help the Cuban crisis. (The other two agencies were the United States Catholic Conference and the Church World Service.) In 1959, HIAS set up operations in Miami for the sole purpose of rescuing Jews fleeing Cuba's revolution. Since Anita was living in New York, she went to the HIAS office located in Manhattan. A permanent visa was denied but they were able to assist our mother in receiving a visa waiver.

Among participating countries, a typical visa waiver allows one to travel for business or tourism and is only good for ninety days; however, these were different. This was a US waiver issued by their representative, the Swiss embassy. It granted many Cuban refugees the ability to flee the oppressive Castro regime, part of a resettlement program initiated by

President Kennedy during his first month of office. With this in hand and her exit permit from the Cuban Ministry of the Interior, she was allowed to leave. Once on US soil, she was granted "indefinite voluntary departure". This was another clever machination devised by the US in an attempt to hasten residency status for Cuban émigrés. Eventually, mama was able to become a permanent resident and then citizen of the United States.

Meanwhile, my father stayed in Havana, trying to sell his clothing shop. It was during the spring of 1963, another ordinary workday for my father. As he approached the store, one of Castro's militiamen was standing by the door. He told my father that he was under orders to confiscate the shop. The soldier went on to explain that the government decided to be generous and allow him to work in the shop. In reality, they wanted my father to show them the ins and outs of the business. My father handed him the keys and wished him the best of luck. His life, like countless other hard working, business savvy Cubans went from riches to rags in a sudden moment. He no longer had any desire to remain in Cuba.

My father told me what happened to his shop and that he was ready to leave for good. I had to find him a visa and getting one through HIAS was now extremely difficult. At the time, only two countries were issuing visas: My old pal Mexico, and Spain. Since I was already living in Spain, procuring a Spanish visa was easy. He left Cuba mid-February, 1964, on Cubana de Aviación airline. The flight was Havana to Prague, both communist at the time, with Newfoundland and Madrid the two stops in between. They were not allowed to refuel in the United States or fly over US territory. The airplane had to be a minimum of three miles offshore from US soil. His flight landed in Newfoundland at the St. John's International Airport.

The plane parked on the frozen Canadian tarmac, the temperature a glacial eighteen degrees Fahrenheit. The captain ordered everyone to disembark until they finished refueling. Not expecting to leave the plane until Madrid, my father was in the official dress code of sunny Cuba: loose-fitting, light-wool pants and a short-sleeved *guayabera* of thin linen. He later told me that he nearly froze walking the tarmac from the plane to the terminal.

For some of the passengers, Canada was their final destination, and many ran to the Canadian Mounted Police to request political asylum. My father was grateful he didn't have to do this since he was coming to Spain. After an hour, the plane refueled, the passengers boarded, and my shivering father was on his way to Madrid.

In the meantime, the weather in Madrid was cold as well. I knew my father did not own a coat or cold-weather clothing. He needed something warm to wear. I went to the *Caritas Españolas*, the Catholic Church's official organization in Spain for charity and social relief, instituted by the Spanish Episcopal Conference. At this Caritas, they were giving out clothing for the impoverished, and I picked the best coat I could find. It was dark-gray wool and extended below the knees. I was waiting for my father in arrivals at the Madrid International Airport. When he appeared, I ran over to him, we hugged and I covered his shoulders with that coat.

He stayed at Jose Levi's, a Sephardic Jew who had the only Jewish boarding house in Madrid. I met Ricardo Myer, a German Jew who moved to Spain with his family and was the vice president of the Jewish community of Madrid. He introduced me to Levi after I told him about my father's arrival. Levi didn't charge my father for boarding or for the three daily meals.

My father was a people person and made friends easily. Every day before lunch, he had a couple of beers with his friends in the basement of that boarding house. It was located in downtown Madrid and allowed him the ability to enjoy the city at his leisure. My father was a creature of habit. He showered at noon, went downstairs to a corner bar, and then returned for lunch. It was June, and in only one week, he was to meet the American Consul to obtain a visa to enter the United States.

That day, he had a heart attack while showering. When the people heard the shower running continually, they knocked on the bathroom door to check on him. There was no answer. They broke the door open and found him dead in the bathtub. He was only fifty-eight.

Twenty-Seven

1945: Washington, DC

On August 20, 1945, Maxine Esther Gritz was born in Washington DC. Our mothers were both born in the same Polish town of Dombrowa, but her mother, Lilly, also known as Laiche, entered the United States by way of Canada.

1932: The Polish passport of my mother-in-law, Lilly (Laiche Schlachter) Gritz.

The two old friends hadn't seen each other in forty years. When my mother arrived in the United States in 1962, she began looking up her childhood friends from Poland. My brother-in-law, Ralph, met the Gritz family in Washington DC and found out that Lilly Gritz, or "Laiche Schlachter", as she was known in their childhood, was one of my mother's best friends from Poland. At long last, the two ladies finally met on July 4, 1963, in Washington DC. It was then that my mother and Laiche renewed their friendship. It was also there that my mother met Mrs. Gritz's daughter, Maxine Esther.

My mother, Sara (Sorche) Shuman, and
Maxine's mother, Lilly (Laiche) Gritz.

Maxine and I became pen pals, corresponding for one year between Spain and Washington DC. In 1964, I was on vacation from medical school and stayed with my sister, Anita, at her apartment in New York. The first time I visited Maxine was July 4, 1964. I took a New England Trailways bus from Port Authority, New York, to Washington DC. Maxine had just gotten her driver's license earlier that year. Her parents bought her a light-blue Nash Rambler.

Maxine in 1963.

Maxine picked me up from the bus station in that Rambler. It was love at first sight. We were married August 29, 1964. After that, Maxine returned with me to Spain.

That was also a sad time for me due to my father's demise in February 1964. He had left Cuba via Spain in February 1964 and died suddenly from a massive heart attack, only a week before he was to meet the American Consul to obtain a visa to enter the United States. He was buried in Paramus, New Jersey.

August 29, 1964: Our Wedding

Maxine and I were newly engaged. The plan was either that I would go back to Spain, and we would get married after a year, or we would get married right away, and then go to Spain together. Adding to the uncertainty of my future was the overwhelming number of new family members. My mother's family consisted of three: my mother, her sister (my aunt, Freidel, or Freida in Spanish), and her brother (my uncle, Chaim), who died before I was born. Compared to my family, Maxine's maternal side, the Hein family was enormous, and after glad-handling future uncles, tantes, brother- and sisters-in-laws, cousins, and other relations from the old country, I was in a daze.

Maxine and I didn't want to wait a whole year, so without hesitation, her mother prepared the wedding with six weeks' notice.

My mother-in-law was a member of the Agudath Achim Congregation in the District of Columbia, and it was a perfect place for our wedding. I wore a white tuxedo with the requisite black bow tie. Maxine looked like a princess in her gown. We stood under a *chuppah* with Rabbi H. Jonah Waldman officiating. Beyond that, the night was a blur, but there are some specifics I do remember. Maxine's brother, Sidney, and his wife, Sandy, were pregnant with their third child, Susie.

Our wedding, 1964

I also keenly remember Maxine's Uncle Moe. He was a short, pudgy man with thick glasses, who always had a cigar in his mouth and was proud of his communist views. He engaged me in nervous conversation.

He knew I had escaped Castro, and he made a point to avoid discussing his politics with me, but I was always worried he might broach the topic.

Our honeymoon was in a motel in downtown Washington DC, and from there, we went to New York City and stayed with my sister, Anita, in the Bronx. The final leg of our journey took place in September; a flight back to Spain with my new wife.

Twenty-Eight

1966: Cadiz, Spain

On January 1, 1966, Ian, our first son, was born in Cadiz, Spain. He was a cute blond baby boy who weighed seven and a half pounds at birth. Maxine was ill with her early pregnancy—she had pernicious vomiting that occurred four or five times a day. She was too sick to fly home to DC to have the baby. Around her seventh month, she had to renew her Spanish visa. The government required her to travel to any nearby country and have the visa stamped; then it would allow reentry. The closest country was Gibraltar, a tiny peninsula of land jutting from the southeast tip of Spain. It is nearly seventy-five miles from Cadiz (and only twenty nautical miles from Morocco). The terrain was rough and hilly, and many of the roads were unpaved. We took a ninety-minute bus ride that was uneven and bumpy- Maxine thought she would go into early labor.

Once we arrived at the Gibraltar border, an immigration officer at the entry point wouldn't allow me to enter with my Cuban visa, US student visa, or green card. I even showed him my US reentry permit. It looked just like an American passport, but the color was dark blue, unlike the traditional passport, which was light blue. This gentleman looked at my documents, raised his head, and said in matter-of-fact terms that he recently went on a trip to the United States and was denied entry. He continued that since he was denied entry to the United States, he would deny me entry into Gibraltar. According to him, I was *un hombre sin patria*, a man without a country.

Maxine, who was already sick from the bus ride, was now disgusted with this man's attitude. A pregnant woman can be fierce. She stepped up to him and said "Do two wrongs make a right?" followed by, "I'm pregnant, and I need my husband's help." Amazingly, this guy backed down and allowed us entry for two hours. We bought American cream cheese and a Scrabble game, and went to the Chief Rabbi for a visit. We returned to Spain with Maxine's renewed visa.

Six months before Ian was born, Maxine had a premonition that we were having a boy and that we would need a mohel. We contacted the German-born Richard M. Mayer Morgenthau who was head of the Jewish community in Madrid. Our correspondence was limited to mail, and typical of the Spanish, his was written in a highly formal, gracious, and kind manner.

Richard had immigrated to Spain several years after World War II. Seeing that we were a young couple without local family, he invited us for Passover. We stayed at the Levi Pension, the same boarding house in which my father died several years earlier. It was the most interesting Seder, with Jews hailing from around the world. There must have been five or six languages spoken at the table, and Max, his wife, and three teenage children spoke each one. He recommended we contact Mr. Isaac Chocrón, a mohel who lived in Tetuan, Morocco. Being the closest available mohel, he was brought over whenever a bris was going to be performed. I contacted the mohel by mail, and he said he was honored and excited to receive a letter from a father-to-be who was preparing for the eventuality of a boy. The following two documents are letters (translated from Spanish) from Richard M. Mayer Morgenthau and Mr. Isaac Chocrón:

Richard M. Mayer Morgenthau
Guzman el Bueno. 2

Madrid, August 07, 1965

Sr. D. José Shuman
Grupo Estadio 2°
/Atico D. Derecha/
CADIZ.-

Dear Friend:

I have received your letter the 4th of August and you will allow me to congratulate you with such wonderful news.

I hope everything will go well to the end and it will be a boy. In this case I can see a few difficulties, because as you know regarding the circumcision ceremony you need 10 men and I doubt very much that where you are now will be 10 Jewish men. However, you have them in Malaga, where there exists a small Sefardi Community, almost all of them from Morocco, and their address is:

Sr. D. Marcos Bedayan
Mármoles, núm. 20
Málaga.-

The "Moel" that we trust is:

Mr. Isaac Chocrón
O'' Donnell, 9.
TETUAN.-

And for the Moel service you shouldn't have to pay for more than his travel expenses.

To make the story short the only solution that I see is as follows:

1°.- Your wife should come to Madrid to give birth and following that 8 days later they will do the circumcision.
2°.- After your wife has given birth and is fully recovered, you can travel with her to Málaga, Tetuan or Tangiers in order to do the circumcision, but in this case you cannot observe the 8 days.

I hope that I have served you correctly with all of this information.

I went with my wife in May on a GOODWILL-MISSION to Cuba to study the situation of the 2,400 people of our faith that still remain over there. We will talk about this particular subject when we will meet again.

And without any further ado, I take this opportunity to congratulate you once again and to send you our warmest regards.

Richard

ISAAC CHOCRÓN SANANES
MOHAM-MED V. 23
TETUAN.

Tetuan December 23 1965

Mr: Don Jose Shuman Cadiz
Dear Sir: Shuman, after I received your letter I am rushing to answer you no matter if your offspring is a girl or a boy.

In regard to my fees this is something that I wouldn't let worry you, my norm is not to demand anything, only my traveling expenses as well as my accommodations in my destination, that shouldn't be more than three days, regarding my fees, my clients pay whatever their economic situation calls for.

Mr: Schuman, it will be a great pleasure to meet you personally with G-d's help and that your desires should be fulfilled. I am now waiting for your good news, I put myself at your disposal and it should be BESIMAN-TOB.

Isaac C.

Ian was due on a Shabbos, and sure enough, on Saturday, January 1, 1966, he was delivered at the Catholic Mora Hospital in Cadiz. Maxine was on the second floor, the VIP area for private patients, and she was the only patient on that floor. It was because she was American, and I was a medical student. They referred to us as *Don Jose y Doña Maxine*, Lord Joseph and Lady Maxine.

Unlike the major hospitals in Spain, this one was small and private. Instead of large numbers of meals delivered to the rooms by an orderly, the Catholic Mora Hospital had a communal kitchen. There, families cooked meals for the infirmed, and brought them to the rooms themselves. Maxine, who was keeping kosher, bought a pan that we kept in a separate part of the kitchen. The nuns were informed of her special diet, but there was one nun who told me that she was planning on cooking non-kosher meat and serving it to Maxine. When I told Maxine of her plans, Maxine said:

"You tell the sister that the sin will be on her, not me".

I informed the sister of Maxine's thoughts on the matter, and the nun laughed and said she was just kidding.

Just to give an idea of the primitive nature of the Catholic Mora Hospital, the delivery room lacked air conditioning, and the nun-midwives swatted the flies that entered the open windows. In those days, in that country, their version of a sterile environment lagged behind the United States (by centuries). Spinal anesthesia mixed with Demerol, a narcotic painkiller, was routinely used during labor and delivery. When Maxine awoke, Ian was on the adjacent bed, and the staff was attending to him. She was restricted to bed for five days. She told the doctor that in America, they let the women out of bed the next day.

"Madam," the doctor said, "this is Spain."

Maxine was released from the hospital on a Thursday. That day, Rabbi Chocrón arrived. Maxine prepared his meals, and he stayed in a small hotel one block from our flat. He brought wine, salami, and matzah. He refused money because I was a student, and it was a mitzvah to do a bris. He asked if we would also be performing a *Pidyon-Haben*, the Redemption of the Firstborn. This law only applies to the other Israelite tribes and not to our family. Traditional history through the generations let us know that we were *Leviim*, Levites, that special tribe responsible for playing music in the temple and tending to the priests.

Before the bris, the parents must choose a name for the baby. In the Ashkenazy eastern European tradition, we name after those who have passed in order to honor these loved ones. Having lost my father only a few years prior, it was an easy choice to name the baby after my father Isaac. His Hebrew name was Yitzchak, but we wanted to give him an English name as well. The big name in the news was the former prime minister of Rhodesia, Ian Smith. His name was pronounced "Eeyan" but we decided to use the long "I" as in "Eye-an", pronounced with the same long "I" as Isaac.

Now, with name-in-hand, it was the day of the bris ceremony. The rabbi brought his traditional surgical instruments soaked in alcohol. I asked if he was going to sterilize them. He said that twenty-four hours in alcohol was more than enough. That wasn't good enough for me. I asked if he wouldn't mind boiling them in water first, and then soaking the instruments in alcohol. He said, "Have it your way," and that's exactly what I did.

He wrapped Ian on a bris board with a swaddling cloth brought from Morocco. The cloth had Hebrew writing and symbols all over it that Maxine later discovered was Kabbalistic incantations. He also performed a uniquely Sephardic ceremony by waving leaves over our baby boy while chanting prayers and making *brachot,* special Hebrew blessings. It was my job to be sandek, the most honored position, where the baby is put on one's lap while holding the legs steady. But I had to look away. Hearing my firstborn cry was one thing, but watching the procedure was more than I could take. Plus, I was, and am still squeamish about certain things, and having nearly passed out at my nephew Milton's bris, I thought that closing my eyes was the better part of discretion; there is no valor in passing out at your own son's bris. Once over, I breathed a deep sigh and craved a cigarette. I don't know who was more relieved: Maxine, the baby, or me.

Dr. Zerolo, my professor and the obstetrician who delivered Ian, was amazed that a non-surgeon had performed the bris. Rabbi Chocrón told us that when he was twenty-five years old, his father, also a mohel, put the knife in his hand and said, "You are doing this bris, and I will be watching you perform it." Rabbi Chocrón stayed an additional two days, changing Ian's bandages. Maxine remembers him peeling an orange in a precise fashion and felt better that he knew what he was doing.

To show what a small world we live in, it was many years later that I attended a medical meeting. We were eating lunch, and everyone wore his or her conference ID badges. One young man had the last name Chocrón. "Where are you from?" I asked.

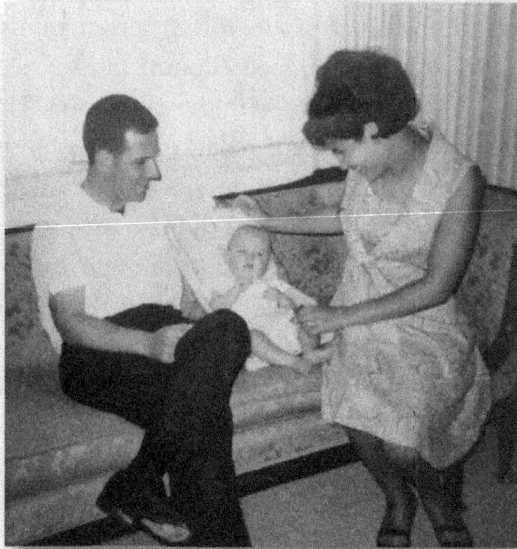

Ian at age 4 months in Cadiz, Spain

"Venezuela," he said.

"The mohel who performed my son's bris was Rabbi Chocrón," I said.

"That was my uncle, and he moved to Israel several years after. Other members of my family moved to Venezuela."

Ian's birth and bris was an historical event. This was due to the fact that he was born to two verified Jewish parents. From the edict of the Spanish Inquisition in 1492 till Dec 31, 1965, there were Jews born in Cadiz, however, one parent was either Catholic, or the parents were Conversos. These children, descendants of baptized Jews, were suspected of secret adherence to Judaism. However, according to Jewish law, their "Jewishness" was suspect.

My brother-in-law Ralph researched the publicized birth of full Jews in Spain, and more specifically the town of Cadiz. After some digging, Ian's birth and bris in Cadiz, Spain, was the first since the Spanish

Inquisition of 1492. This was corroborated by several historians and the event made the newspapers, including the popular Yiddish papers, The Forward and The Day.

The Day – Jewish Journal
Tuesday, January 4, 1966
First Jewish Boy Born In Southern Spain
Since The Inquisition

Special news from the newspaper "The Day"

Cadiz, Spain, January 3 – Here yesterday was born the first Jewish child, a boy, since the Spanish Inquisition.

The child was born to the happy parents, Mr. and Mrs. Shuman. The father, Joseph Shuman, was born in Cuba and is studying medicine in a school in Cadiz. The mother was born in

America, in Washington, DC, and her maiden name is Maxine
Gritz.

The mother gave birth in a Catholic hospital and the nuns
were told that she was not allowed to eat treif and were told what
she was allowed to eat.

In order to circumcise the child, a mohel will come especially
from Morocco. The Shumans are the only Jewish family in Cadiz.

On January 20, 1966, Rabbi Zev K. Nelson, a pulpit Rabbi of Temple
Emeth in Chestnut Hill, Massachusetts, was so moved by the event, that
he published a *dvar Torah,* a sermon relating to that weeks Torah portion. His weekly news column in The Jewish Advocate, "Just A Thought"
was entitled "Keeping The Covenant".[6] He wrote:

"A recent news release in the Anglo-Jewish press told of the birth of
a Jewish boy in Cadiz, Spain. What made it newsworthy was the fact that
this was the first Jewish child born in southern Spain since the expul-
sion of 1492. Yet there was another aspect to it that was perhaps more
significant. Mr. and Mrs. Joseph Shuman, the happy parents of the new-
born infant, are the only Jews in Cadiz. They are there because Joseph
Shuman is studying medicine at the University of Cadiz.

Two important things happened when the baby was born. The nuns
of the Catholic hospital in Cadiz provided Mrs. Shuman with special
food, which, she as a Jewess, could eat. What is even more noteworthy,
the Shumans arranged to have a Mohel come from Morocco to perform
the circumcision and bring the child into the covenant of Abraham.
Apparently, the medical student was not content with a surgical circumcision performed by a doctor. The mother and father, alone in Cadiz,
wanted to make sure their child would be a true son of his people, initiated into its tradition from the days of his infancy. It is equally apparent
that the Catholic nuns of Cadiz have high regard for Jews who have the
courage of their convictions and seek to abide by their faith.

---

6 Nelson, Zev K. "Keeping The Covenant". "Just A Thought" *The Jewish Advocate,* Boston, MA.
January 20, 1966.

This week's *Sidra* of *Vaera*, brings us the divine call to freedom, with the well-known refrain: 'Let my people go, that they may serve Me.' God calls them His people, because they are prepared to serve Him. They are worthy of liberation, because they are willing to keep the covenant and remain the people of God.

It is not easy always to serve God and to keep His commandments. But, whether expelled from Spain, or alone in Spain, one must have a sense of purpose, a feeling of dedication and a willingness to serve God – and then all difficulties are overcome – then you no longer look for an easy way out, but you seek the right way into the fold of Israel."

On our balcony in Cadiz, Spain, June 1966

But no amount of historical fame could keep Ian healthy as an infant. His first few months of life were marked by constant respiratory and ear infections. The pediatrician suggested that we move to a less humid climate. We followed his advice, and with an opportunity to switch to a new medical school, we moved to Salamanca. This city is in northwestern Spain, near the Portuguese border. Ian thrived in the cool, dry weather and his medical problems were soon gone. We stayed in Salamanca for a year, and in June 1967 I graduated medical school from the University of Salamanca. I was elated. Finally, I was a doctor.

Twenty-Nine

1967: Ravenna, Ohio

After graduation, we moved back to America. I completed my internship from June 1, 1967, to July 1, 1969, at Robinson Memorial Hospital in Ravenna, Ohio. It was a small facility with just over two hundred beds. The ICU had no more than ten beds. As a comparison, average-sized hospitals have well over fifty ICU beds, and those are distributed throughout different departments.

The hospital was on Meridian Street, and it served all of Portage County. Ravenna was a small town and didn't even have a movie theater. For that, we went to the closest movie house located in Kent. In fact, the hospital was located only ten miles from Kent State University, the site of the infamous 1970 Kent State shooting. The closest large city was Akron, a twenty-one-mile drive, where Maxine traveled to buy kosher meat.

Myself and another man (whose name I forget) were the only Jews in Ravenna, Ohio. This "other man" owned a haberdashery on Main Street. When he told us his name, we discovered he was Jewish.

At the age of twenty-six, I enrolled in a local driving school, got my license and bought my first car from the Ravenna GM dealership. It was the only place in town to buy a car. It was an eight-cylinder, four-door 1968 Chevy Chevelle Malibu. It had a sky-blue roof, a metallic-blue body, and cost $2,700. It had AM/FM radio with an eight-track tape deck and white-wall tires that were both optional. I put down $500 and financed the rest. Even though gas was twenty-five cents a gallon, it drank fuel *como un niño bobo*, like a stupid kid. Shoulder seat belts were the newest requirement to be installed in these cars, but no one ever put them on.

I hated them; they were too restrictive. We bought a child seat, but it wasn't for safety. The seat was elevated so two-year-old Ian could look out the window.

1969: Baltimore, Maryland

After Ravenna, we moved to Baltimore, Maryland where I completed my medical residency at the Greater Baltimore Medical Center (GBMC) and Sinai Hospital. During this time, Maxine was pregnant with our second child. Anticipating a dead-of-winter delivery, we made plans to leave Ian with a babysitter. As luck would have it, I was friendly with Dr. Alberto Gutiérrez, a fellow Cuban and chief resident in OBGYN at GBMC. He and his wife Edith lived in a building only a short walk from ours, in Cockeysville on Lord Byron Lane. Alberto was fourteen years my senior and already a highly skilled physician. Trained in Cuba, he was required to repeat some medical school and a full residency. It was true dedication. This wonderful couple told us that they would be happy to have Ian stay with them when Maxine was in labor. "Any time of day or night, don't hesitate to knock on our door," they told us.

O January 1, 1970, Maxine went into labor at 1:00 am. We packed some things, and I picked up Ian to carry him to the Gutiérrez'. There was heavy snow on the ground. I slipped and fell, but I held Ian so he wouldn't get hurt. Ian fell on my chest and I had a sore backside. The couple babysat Ian and we headed for GBMC. Upon arrival, Maxine was checked in. She was whisked away to labor and delivery, and I whisked myself to the men's room. After washing up and changing into a pair of scrubs, I was escorted into the delivery room where one of the physicians from the Engelhardt and Peterson OB team was delivering the baby. Making it in the nick of time, I watched the birth of a beautiful, seven-pound baby boy. We named him Michael Frederick, Michael Ephraim, named after Maxine's great aunt Mary and her grandmother, (Sarah) Fraydel.

Amazingly, Michael and Ian were now born on the same day, exactly four years apart. Maxine was in the hospital for three days. We brought

Michael home and Ian couldn't wait to see him. When Ian held Michael, he was the most excited child Maxine and I had ever seen. Ian even wanted to change his brothers' diapers. By then, disposable diapers were available, a far cry from Ian's hand washed diapers that went from the bathtub, to dry on the radiator and then be ironed.

Michael was always very well behaved. He loved sports and would read the sport statistics at age five. His ability to memorize things of interest was uncanny. When Ian was in the sixth grade, he had to memorize all the capitals of the US. Michael was in the room listening to Maxine and I quizzing Ian. I asked Ian the capital of Oregon. He thought hard, but couldn't come up with the answer. After some time, Michael quietly spoke.

"I know the capital of Oregon", he said. "It's Salem".

On a whim, we decided to test six-year-old Michael on the capitals. Amazingly, he had memorized them all.

Michael was always easy-going. As a kid, he was charismatic, made many friends, and was loved by everyone. Today, Michael is a middle school math teacher and is loved by his students, their parents and the faculty. He is also a highly sought after tutor, and is now spearheading a foundation called Footsteps of Our Fathers where he takes groups to Eastern Europe, recounting the atrocities of the holocaust. He is married to Miriam (Micky) Greenberg and together they have four children: Alexandra, Jessica, Samantha, and Matthew.

1971: Pittsburgh, Pennsylvania

From Baltimore, we moved to Pittsburgh, Pennsylvania, where I attended a fellowship in endocrinology at Montefiore Hospital University of Pittsburgh School of Medicine. During the winter of 1972, there was a particularly nasty bug going around. Naturally, I caught it, (probably from ill patients in the hospital) and Michael and Ian soon followed. It was called the London flu and it was responsible for many deaths, especially the very old and young. We remained "quarantined" on a pull-out sofa bed in the living room of our tiny apartment. Maxine, who was nursing us back to health, was also pregnant with our third child, coincidentally due on January 1, 1973.

At first, she seemed fine, but the aggressive virus caused her to develop a severe bronchitis with deep coughing fits. The coughing had put her into early labor and she was rushed to McGee Women's Hospital. On December 13, 1972, Maxine gave birth to a six pound, two ounce, gorgeous baby girl. We named her Miriam Ahuva after Maxine's uncle Moe (my favorite cigar chomping socialist).

L. to R.: Michael age 3, Maxine, Ian age 7, and me holding Miriam age 1

Two weeks later, I left to Florida for a prospective job interview at a private practice in Broward General Hospital. While away, Maxine's cough worsened. I arranged for her to see an internist at my residency hospital, Dr. Phillip Brostoff. He diagnosed her with pneumonia and asked Maxine if she had anyone to take care of the baby? In tears, Maxine informed him that she now had three little ones, all under the age of seven, and that she was alone while I was away in Florida. Maxine told him that her mother and sister were coming that night to see the new baby. When Laiche arrived, Maxine was running a high fever.

Laiche called Dr. Brostoff and said she thought that Maxine should go to the hospital. The doctor said there is no one better to care for a child than his or her mother. So Laiche and Marlene cared for Maxine, baby Miriam, and the boys.

Miriam was a quiet, good-natured baby. She looked like a little porcelain doll and Ian and Michael loved her. Miriam had dark curly hair and deep cherry black eyes. She favored my mother's side of the family being petite, but favored the Hein side of Maxine's family in terms of looks. A gorgeous girl, she excelled in school, and had many close, loyal friends who are still in touch with each other, despite the fact that most of them have moved to Israel. She went to college on early admissions, attending Machon Gold, a seminary for young women in Jerusalem. Her year was cut short due to the Gulf War and she returned home. She went on to complete her education at Touro College, NY, earning a bachelors degree in education. She is married to Eli Jacobs and together, they have five children: Rina, Abie, Talia, Ezra, and Leah.

1973: North Miami Beach, Florida

The job prospect trip to Florida had paid off. I really wanted a warm climate, a reminder of the Havana heydays. With the large Cuban population of South Florida, oftentimes, I felt at home. There, I settled into private practice and made rounds at the local hospitals. On November 11, 1976, our fourth child was born at North Miami General Hospital. It was a baby girl, and she weighed 7 pounds at birth. We named her Shira Elka, after Maxine's grandfather Sam and my maternal grandmother. Coincidentally, Nov 11th is Maxine's mothers' birthday and amazingly, Shira looks very much like her maternal grandmother.

Shira was a handful, constantly on the move. She would creep to the other end of her crib at five days old. Back then, babies were placed on their stomachs and Leiche told Maxine to remove blankets or anything else that might cover Shira's head. Nothing could hold Shira down, and she walked at ten months of age. She loved to teach imaginary classes, and would line up her dolls on chairs, have a child sized blackboard, and

L. to R. Shira age 2, Miriam 6, Michael 9, Ian 13

would teach them the ABC's, reading, and sing songs. She would also dance at home all throughout the house and acted in school plays. Like her sister Miriam, she went early admission, and graduated with a degree in education from Touro College. She is married to Binny (Barry) Hahn and together, they have six children: Elisheva, Orly, Mia, Shai, Daniella, and Zahava.

Thirty

The Move to Israel

Maxine visited Israel in 1963, and loved it there. She always desired to spend more time in Israel or move there. She was Zionistic. I wasn't as die-hard, but Cuban Jews were very pro-Israel, and I remember sending clothing and money to the young fledgling country. And that's how I was brought up—with a deep feeling of Zionism. But we weren't moving anywhere since Spain, medical school, and then internship and residency took up life.

In 1972, I was doing my fellowship in Pittsburgh. The University of Pittsburgh gave us an annual free trip to any medical convention in endocrinology at the school's expense. Israel was hosting an international meeting in endocrinology and I told the University sponsors that I wanted to go to the Israeli meeting. They asked if there wasn't a closer meeting, but I talked them into it. The meeting was held outside Tel Aviv—*Bitan Aharon*, where they would accommodate all the attendees and had a special meeting hall with rooms like a country inn. The meeting was three to four days.

I called Maxine from Israel, and I was so enthused about what I saw there and how they practiced medicine, and I asked her, "How would you like to move here?"

"Are you crazy?" she said. "I'm pregnant, and due next month."

After the meeting the conference organizers took the American attendees on excursions to Tel Aviv and Jerusalem in an attempt to promote the country. After visiting these beautiful cities, I went off on my own to see my uncle Boruch and aunt Freidel.

They immigrated from Cuba directly to a small one-bedroom apartment in the city of Bat Yam, Israel, We talked a lot about the county, and that I was keen on living in Israel. In his deep baritone voice, Boruch said, "I want you to know that life in Israel is very nice but very hard!" His warning would be prophetic.

Back in the United States, Maxine and I discussed moving to Israel more seriously, but that desire was put on ice for several more years. In 1973 we moved to South Florida, where I started practicing. When the subject of Israel came up again, in the late 1970s, I was turning forty and felt that it was the right age to make the move.

We made an appointment with the *Misrad Haaliyah*, the office for new immigration in downtown Miami Beach. The *shaliach*, or emissary, was an Israeli man who was the local director for potential immigrants. He recommended I go on a pilot trip before making any decisions. I went to New York to the Israeli *aliyah* office, and they had organized a plane expressly for the pilot tour. We boarded a 707 Pan Am airplane and flew New York to Rome, and then Rome to Israel. On that trip, I met a fellow doctor, an oncologist named Tommy Tischler. We became instant friends. He was practicing in Chicago, had recently married and had saved enough money to settle in Israel and build a house there. Not having the funds to build or buy a home in Israel, I spoke to the office for new *olim* to find out what living arrangements were available.

The shaliach said the economy there was not great. At that time, the Israeli government was under the tenure of Prime Minister Menachem Begin who put a freeze on all government hiring. It also meant that the aliyah office was not supposed to help anyone get a government job. Despite this, the aliyah office had secured a job for me at the military based Tel Hashomer Hospital, with the possibility that the job could become permanent. In addition, we would be provided temporary housing at a *mercaz klitah*, an absorption center. So we packed up and moved to Israel.

When we arrived, we went to a mercaz klitah located in the hills of Mevaseret Tzion, nine miles south of Jerusalem. We arrived in the summer, but when the winter came, we quickly discovered that the homes

The kids in Israel.
Ian 14, Michael 10, Mi   riam 7, Shira 3

there were not insulated. Since Mevaseret Tzion was nestled in the high country, the blowing wind was constant. Meanwhile, our money proceeds from the sale of our house in Florida was quickly draining. With scant funds, I was growing anxious. In Israel, you can't do much with an anemic bank account, and by American standards, my Israeli salary was small. Eventually, I required overdrafts for an entire month's salary. We lived on overdrafts, nonexistent money, and I couldn't continue living like this. This was not how I was brought up, and I told Maxine I was not going to go on this way.

So after two years, I said, "Let's be realistic about this. We won't be able to make it here. Doctors' salaries are terrible, and who is going to pay for our kids' college educations?" No government subsidies existed for Israeli college tuition. Maxine was upset. She was a hoper, a dreamer, saying God would help. My salary was $350 and we were spending about $500 a month in the supermarket. That didn't take into account clothing and other basics. My Uncle Boruch was right. Things in Israel did not go as smoothly as we wanted or anticipated. The country itself met our expectations; however, supporting a family of four children became an uphill battle. Financially it was a disaster and we needed to find a place where we could live without constant economic struggle.

Reluctantly, we returned to the United States.

Thirty-One

1982: Returning to the States

While in Israel, Maxine and I were planning our move back to the US. I wanted to return to Florida and start my own practice. I knew enough people who would help me settle again. So, packing up again, we returned to the United States. Maxine and the kids stayed at Laiches' in Maryland while I sought prospects in Miami.

My childhood friend from Cuba, Sarita Milkis (who also lived in North Miami Beach) put me in touch with her best friend's husband, a cardiologist who had a local practice. He had space for me in his office in order to see my own patients. Maxine and the kids flew down to join me in our new life. We rented an apartment in the Sussex House just off Dixie Highway, near Lorenzo's fruit-and-vegetable market. It was a nice apartment, spacious, with enough room for everyone. However, Maxine wasn't thrilled with the location because there wasn't a *shul* within walking distance of the apartment.

In 1983, we decided to buy a house on 173 Street, where we still live. I moved to a new practice owned by a Jewish-Cuban general physician where I practiced general medicine and was paid a salary. I was still determined to be my own boss with a practice of my own. In those times, a doctor's signature was all that was required to secure a loan. So I signed for a bank loan that was payable over five years. I paid it off in three.

April 1990: The March of the Living

It seems that in life, everything comes full circle. Despite the death of family members murdered in the holocaust and the tenacious nature of my people, life returned to the death camps of Treblinka and Auschwitz. Each year, groups are organized to visit these sites and proudly demonstrate that we, the Jewish people, are very much alive and well.

In April, 1990, we joined one such group: The March of the Living. Maxine was working at the Hillel Academy Jewish Day School, and the students were an important part of the march that year. Maxine was going and asked me to come along. We went as chaperones and I as a doctor for the group. We flew from Miami International Airport to John F. Kennedy Airport in New York. From there, we flew on the Polish national Lott Airlines directly to Warsaw. As *madrichim* (the Hebrew word for chaperones), we were lucky to be given first-class seats.

Upon arrival, we checked in at a hotel in Warsaw and then shuttled to Mila 18, a bunker that in 1943 was used as headquarters by Jewish resistance fighters. The resistance fighters hid underneath the building at Ulica Miła 18, a.k.a. 18 Mila, or "Pleasant Street" in Polish. This site was made famous by the novel *Mila 18* by Leon Uris.

Later that day, we had time off to recuperate from the long flight. We were explicitly told not to wander around Warsaw because tourists were frequently mugged in the streets. Of course, we did the opposite. Maxine had to buy postcards to update the family on our progress. Now she sends e-mails, but then, that was not an option. So we wandered by ourselves to the post office, and using a combination of sign language and English, we bought cards without a problem and returned safely to our hotel.

Later that evening, we rode the elevator down to the lobby for dinner. In our elevator car were several Polish men who were chatting in Polish about our kids and their *kippot*. One of our Polish-fluent chaperones told us that these men said, "We thought we got rid of them." That was the mind-set of our host country. People were still transfixed on the "Jewish" element that they thought were exterminated. It was precisely for that reason that we were in that country with pride in our hearts and minds. Yes, we were still alive and back to view the carnage of history that left so many of our family dead.

The next day, we began our march by arriving at the death and forced-labor camp of Auschwitz. We saw the famous *"arbeit macht frei"* wrought-iron fence. The Nazis were clever in deceit, and the true nature of their macabre plans was known to only a few. However, it was impossible for the local peasants and farmers who surrounded these camps to not know the true nature of places like Auschwitz. It was recounted by so many eyewitnesses: it constantly "rained" ashes for miles, the result of cremating millions of Jews, gypsies, and other 'undesirables." They knew the train schedule ran like a finely made precision clock, cattle cars stuffed with corpses and terrified victims, exhausted from the long, deadly trips.

Separated by only a few miles, we marched from Auschwitz to Birkenau and, from there, were shuttled to the Treblinka death camp located on the outskirts of Warsaw. It was widely known that Treblinka was a one-way ticket to the crematoria, and using another twisted tactic of deceit, the Nazis placed a huge Star of David over the gas chamber. It was meant to look like a *mikvah*, the Jewish ritual bath used for purification of the soul. Unfortunately, the one million souls who perished would never need a mikvah again. Their souls were forever purified as unwilling martyrs under Nazi murder.

We marched on other camps in Krakow (Krakow-Plaszow) and Lublin (Majdanek). The Polish citizens all denied knowing there was a concentration camp in Lublin. Smoke spewed from the crematoria, the stench of burning bodies filled the air, and ash fell all around. How could they not know?

The March of the Living traveled from the death camps of Poland to lively, tumultuous Tel Aviv, Israel. On the Polish airfield, we boarded an all-white unmarked EL AL airplane to avoid arousing acts of terror. Polish and Israeli guards were posted on the tarmac next to the plane and patrolled the area where we waited. It was a trip I will never forget.

Epilogue

For the reader who has gone through this book, you will notice that the various story's and accounts cover many violent chapters in modern history including WWI, the pogroms of Eastern Europe, the Russian Revolution, WW II, Batista's coup d'état, Castro's communist revolution, and the era of the Cuban Missile Crisis, among others. These were significant world events that my family and I had actually experienced. This brings me to the most current event, the newly minted US-Cuban foreign relations.

Even though the relations were broken in 1960, they are now trying to mend it slowly and gradually and what that means for the future is uncertain. The Cubans are divided according to age. Those from my generation who still remember Castro's early days are vehemently against it. The current generation is for it. The US has given Cuba all they have requested including diplomatic relations and open travel between the two countries. In return, the Cuban government has not given their citizenry the basic rights enjoyed by many countries including the freedom of speech, the right to vote, and open commerce. This chapter has yet to be written.

I am now seventy-six years old and trying to decide if and when to retire. I still enjoy practicing medicine in my specialty of endocrinology. The big question is, how long will I be able to carry on, and what will I do after retirement? Writing these memoirs has been first and foremost in my mind. Perhaps more books will follow.

Author Biography

Dr. Joseph Shuman, MD, was born and raised in Havana, Cuba, where he lived during the 1940s and 1950s. He immigrated to the United States shortly after Fidel Castro seized power.

A practicing endocrinologist for forty-two years, he has called Miami home since 1973. He and his wife, Maxine, have been married for fifty-one years and have twenty-one grandchildren.